108+ High Quality Passive Income Ideas

By Adara Parker

As a token of my gratitude for your recent purchase, I'm excited to offer you an exclusive copy of *108+ High Quality Passive Income Ideas* for free.

Get your free copy at bit.ly/108passiveincome.

Inside This Must-Read Guide, You'll Discover:

- **High Quality Passive Income Strategies:** An abundance of high-quality ideas to generate passive income.
- **Automatable Business Ideas:** Learn about various types of businesses that you can start and

automate for efficiency, ensuring a steady flow of income.

- **Smart Investment Ideas:** Explore a variety of investments you can make, as well as user-friendly investing platforms to grow your wealth.

Why You Shouldn't Miss This Opportunity:

- If you're aiming to diversify your income sources and build multiple passive income streams, this book is your key to unlocking those goals.
- Packed with real-world examples and success stories, it's more than just a book, this book suggests what may be uniquely possible for you.

Get Instant Access! Claim your free copy of **108+ High Quality Passive Income Ideas** *at bit.ly/108passiveincome.*

Thank you again for your purchase and I hope you enjoy the book!

THE CHATGPT MILLIONAIRE

TRANSFORM FINANCIAL STRUGGLE INTO
PASSIVE INCOME, OVERCOME YOUR MONEY
BLOCKERS, AND UNLOCK YOUR EARNING
POTENTIAL

ADARA PARKER

ADARA PARKER PUBLISHING

INTRODUCTION

"Whatever you can do, or dream you can, begin it. Bold-
ness has genius, power, and magic in it." — *Johann Wolf-
gang von Goethe*

I wrote this book because I believe that if you want it, you
can become a ChatGPT millionaire in your lifetime.

It's a matter of three things: your state of mind, your
mastery of the technology, and applying these towards an
automatable business that you can scale.

Whether you're a student, an employee, or an
entrepreneur, no matter where you are in your journey, the
path to your dreams is possible today.

I'm a technology entrepreneur who uses ChatGPT every
day. I've led teams that have built end-to-end applications in
production on top of GPT-4. I have the honor of meeting
with engineering leaders from start-ups to Fortune 500
companies daily, working with them to build applications in
production that transform and automate their businesses.

If you're reading this book, chances are there is a leap

you're looking to take, and you're looking for ideas and inspiration on how to do it.

I wrote this book to share what I know about cultivating a millionaire mindset and practical applications of technology. In this book, I also share three automatable business ideas that you can start today.

My intention and vision with this book are for you to be inspired and empowered with states of mind, technical knowledge, and inspiring stories of successful entrepreneurs so that you can take that leap and make your dreams come true.

1

MONEY BLOCKERS

"You have to let go of the things that don't work, and you have to find new things that work." — *My Teacher*

How often do you find yourself saying, 'I don't have any money,' 'I never have enough money,' or something similar?

You are not alone. A survey by GoBankingRates in 2019 indicated that 45% of Americans had nothing saved for retirement. The same study found that 69% of Americans had less than $1,000 in savings. The average student loan debt is $38,000, and the average U.S. household credit card debt is $6,270.

Unsurprisingly, we may feel stuck and like there's no way out regarding money. It's a shared experience of our culture.

Limiting financial beliefs are deeply ingrained thoughts or convictions about money that can hinder one's economic success and overall well-being. These beliefs can come from childhood experiences, societal norms, or past failures.

When you have limiting beliefs in place, you can learn

everything there is to know about stocks, technology, business, and wealth creation. Still, with deeply ingrained limitations about what's possible for you, you may not get the results that you're looking for.

If you can identify the limiting beliefs you regularly believe in, you can begin to let them go or replace them with constructive and expansive beliefs that align with where you want to go.

The Realm of Lack & Limitation

What are limiting beliefs? Limiting beliefs are any beliefs, thoughts, ideas, or feelings restricting what is possible. They could be phrases that you always say, like, "I never have enough" or "That's too expensive."

Many of these beliefs may not even be our own. We may have observed them from our friends, families, culture, and media and immediately agreed with them from a young age without questioning whether we wanted to guide our lives with that belief. Suddenly, we've limited the scope of what we believe is possible.

Let's look at common financial limiting beliefs to identify where we may be holding ourselves back and replace them with constructive beliefs moving forward.

What are examples of common financial limiting beliefs?

"I don't have any money."
"That's too expensive."
"Rich people are bad, greedy, dishonest."
"If I go for the promotion, I'll just be working all the time."
"I'm just not good with money."
"Money is the root of all evil."

"I don't deserve to be wealthy."

"I'll never get out of debt."

"It's selfish to want a lot of money."

"It's too late to change my story."

"I don't need to worry about money; someone else will handle it for me."

"There is never enough."

"Taxes are evil."

"Money doesn't come to me easily."

"Earning money requires working hard."

"Money is made to be spent."

"Money is on its way out the door."

"Making lots of money requires sacrificing who you are."

"Why does this always happen to me?"

"I am unworthy."

"I'm constantly worrying about money."

"More money, more problems."

"Money is hard to get."

Do you think *even one* of these beliefs regularly? You may be putting significant friction on your wheels towards your own goals.

How do limiting beliefs hold us back?

Limiting beliefs acts like invisible barriers, constraining our lives in ways we may not even realize.

First, they can undermine our self-confidence and ability to visualize, connect with, and create meaningful success for ourselves. Operating with limiting beliefs is like never being able to go full-speed towards our goals because it's like driving with friction around our tires.

For example, when you believe "I'm not good enough" or

"I'm not going to be successful" you may be reluctant to try new things or give your total energy and effort towards your endeavors. You're already *believing* that you're going to fail. You're holding back.

Second, they can limit the goals we set for ourselves. If we have decided that specific goals are impossible, we may not even explore what it may take to make them come true for us. We're creating a self-imposed ceiling.

Third, in our careers, we may choose not to go for a promotion or to take on a new challenge because we're afraid we will fail. We may miss income, personal development, and deeply satisfying work.

Letting go of limitation

Limiting beliefs are not real. Our limiting beliefs are just arbitrary ideas that we've decided are true. We may have decided they are true a long time ago without giving it much thought. When you realize that limiting beliefs are just arbitrary ideas that are not true, no longer help us, and that we can let go of, we can begin to transcend them.

Limiting beliefs are not an unchangeable part of who we are. They are learned perceptions; we can just as quickly unlearn them and replace them with more empowering beliefs.

The Realm of Abundance, Prosperity, and Infinite Possibilities

Let's let go of limitation and transition from the realm of lack & limitation into the realm of abundance, prosperity, and infinite possibilities.

America is the land of opportunity for a reason. Did you

know the U.S. has the highest number of millionaires and billionaires worldwide? Specifically, the U.S. has the highest number of millionaires and billionaires who *earned that wealth in their lifetime.*

According to the Credit Suisse Global Wealth Report 2021, the U.S. had over 20 million millionaires, representing approximately 40% of the world's total millionaires.

The U.S. also has the highest number of billionaires worldwide. As per Forbes' 2021 Billionaires List, the U.S. was home to 724 billionaires.

You may wonder, "Those people got a handout; they got an inheritance." Hold your thought for just a second.

According to a 2019 Wealth-X and Fidelity Investments study, two-thirds of millionaires are self-made.

Additionally, a personal finance expert, Dave Ramsey, found that 79% of millionaires did not receive an inheritance from parents or other family members. Instead, they achieved millionaire status through hard work and smart financial choices.

Maybe you're not where you want to be: a millionaire or a billionaire. But the good news is that you have all the resources and examples of people who have already done what you want to do. At least 20 million of them, to be precise.

How to identify and replace your limiting beliefs

Overcoming limiting beliefs is not just about altering your thoughts. It's about changing the narrative of your life. It's about changing the energy with which you go about your day.

In this section, I want to share a structure for overcoming limiting beliefs that I learned from Tony Robbins at a Business Mastery Seminar, which he adapted from Brene Brown.

Here is a constructive way to overcome your limiting beliefs:

1. What limiting belief do you want to let go of?
2. Ask yourself, "Is this really true?" Look for how it's *not true.*
3. What are the consequences of continuing to believe this?
4. How would your life be different without this belief? How would you change? How would your life change?
5. What is a powerful and constructive belief that you could hold instead? Look for ways that this new belief is true. Find evidence for your new belief.
6. What are the constructive consequences of my new belief? What could I do if I knew I could not fail?

What are examples of abundant beliefs?

To balance out the limiting beliefs above, I'd like to include a list of abundant financial beliefs to understand the beliefs you can create for yourself.

"Avalanches of money come to me with joy and ease."
"I am impeccable at managing my finances."
"I am deserving of abundance and prosperity."
"I am skillful."
"I am financially free."
"I am financially independent."
"Wealth and abundance flow to me with joy and ease."
"Everything I touch turns to gold."
"I am a money magnet."

"I deserve to make more money."
"I attract money effortlessly and with ease."
"Money flows openly into my life."
"I am grateful for all the money I have now."
"Attracting money comes easy to me."
"My prosperity is limitless."
"My money works hard for me."
"My actions create prosperity."

I recommend writing beliefs that capture the energy and the essence of who you want to be. Be silly, be goofy, and find ones that feel good. Have fun with it!

3 Tips for Living Your New Beliefs

You wrote down your new beliefs; now what? Here are three tips for operating at your new level. Here are a few other ways you can put structures in your day to perform at the level that you want to be. You can continue to work on turning around your limiting beliefs in a few other ways.

Hour of Power

One of my favorite things is starting my day with my morning Hour of Power. It's an hour that I set aside every morning, first thing in the morning, to reflect, review, and recommit to my goals. I take this time to train my mind and reconnect with who I want to be.

You can design your hour of power (or 35 minutes or 45 minutes) to be what you need to perform at your best. With your hour of power, you can start your day strong, organized, and tracking toward your goals, starting by reconnecting to what matters most.

Here are some things you can schedule in your Hour of Power:

• **Goal Review:** Review the goals that you've set for yourself and reconnect to what it feels like to have achieved that goal. Cover the delta between where you are now and where you need to be to achieve your goals.
• **Reflective Journaling:** Write down your thoughts, successes, and challenges. Looking back at previous journal records from your hour of power and seeing your progress and mindset will be a blessing.
• **Affirmations:** Continue letting go of limiting beliefs by replacing them with constructive, empowering affirmations reinforcing your new beliefs. Begin your day with affirmations that reinforce your new beliefs. This daily practice helps to solidify these beliefs in your mind.
• **Gratitude:** Start your day by connecting with what you are truly thankful for. Gratitude is a practice, not another item on your to-do list. By practicing gratitude and focusing on what we are grateful for, we focus on what is right in our lives.

Doing so allows us to more deeply connect with and experience the abundance and beauty around us and continue to attract more of what is right in our lives.

Mindfulness

Mindfulness is an ongoing daily practice of observing your states of mind, discontinuing negative thoughts, and replacing them with positive, empowering, or constructive thoughts.

Practicing mindfulness lets you catch when you're going

back into deconstructive thought patterns and gently let them go. Letting go of your old state of mind allows you to reconnect with your new state of mind.

You can also limit or let go of negative influences to aid your mindfulness practice. Minimize contact with environments or people that reinforce your old limiting beliefs. Declutter your apartment and let go of items that connect you to your past. Let go of social media or media that creates downward spirals in your attention.

You are not your negative thoughts. You are not your limiting beliefs.

Over time, by practicing mindfulness, you will be able to notice when you have a negative thought and intentionally let it go and replace it with who you want to be.

Setting New Goals

Finally, set new goals that reinforce your new beliefs. Start small, accumulate wins, and build momentum. What small goal can you set to support the believe that *money comes to you with ease and joy*? Please write it down and track that goal in your daily hour of power.

• What goals can you set to reinforce your new beliefs and abilities?

• Write them down and review them in your daily Hour of Power.

• Celebrate the wins! When you've achieved the goal, celebrate!

• Select a new small goal that can further reinforce your new belief and allow you to build more momentum. Write that goal down for review in your daily Hour of Power and continue building the cycle of wins and momentum.

Conclusion

Becoming who we want to be is a continuous process of letting go of what doesn't work and finding what works.

Whether you reside in the land of lack & limitation or abundance, prosperity, and infinite possibilities is up to you.

Your limiting beliefs are not real. They are just ideas you can let go of and replace with more constructive ideas at any time.

America is the land of millionaires and billionaires. Now, more than ever, we have advanced technology at our fingertips to create wealth for ourselves, our families, and our loved ones.

The time is now to make a change. Start by examining your beliefs and choosing goals that align with who you genuinely want to be.

2

MILLIONAIRE MINDSETS

"The key to financial freedom and great wealth is a person's ability to convert earned income into passive and/or portfolio income." — *Robert Kiyosaki*

I n this chapter, I'd like to share some of the most significant personal finance and wealth-building mindsets that opened my eyes to a higher way of building businesses and creating wealth.

Cash Flow Equals Energy Flow

"Cash flow equals energy flow" is a very simple but profound teaching. Your financial well-being and your spiritual well-being are linked. How much money you make meaningfully affects how much energy you have.

The more money you have, the more energy you have. The more money you have, the better you can protect yourself from the difficult energies of the world.

If you're without a job and are not making any money, then getting *any job* and making *any money* is a fast path to lift you into a higher level of personal power. It creates more balance. Even though the initial job you get may not be perfect, the increase in cash flow will increase your energy and personal power and allow you to re-evaluate the right next job for you from a more strategic vantage point.

Do you feel like you might be plateauing? Take a look at your cash flows. Is there something that you can rebalance?

If you're considering a new job, but your new job is going to create less cash flow for you, you may experience a considerable decrease in energy due to the reduction in cash flow.

Increases and decreases in cash flow mirror increases and decreases in personal energy flow.

With this in mind, you can build your energy and personal power by creating increased cash flow. Focusing on building your cash flow is constructive for you materially, spiritually, and energetically.

Higher earnings lead to increased personal power, greatly assisting you with initiatives that can truly help the world.

Assets vs. Liabilities

I first learned about the differences between **assets** and **liabilities** from Robert Kiyosaki's Rich Dad Poor Dad book, which I highly recommend reading along with the remaining books in his Cashflow Quadrant series.

To summarize the key takeaway, an **asset** is anything that *puts money in your pocket*, while a **liability** is anything that *takes money away*.

One of the most significant key takeaways from the book is that many people consider their home an asset, but if your home is not actively generating cash for you, it's not an asset. It's a liability.

Many people spend their energy accumulating liabilities like cars, homes, and various credit card debts, which ultimately drain their resources and energy flow.

In contrast, wealthy individuals concentrate on building and acquiring assets.

Are you focused on building assets, or are you accumulating liabilities? If you look at your personal balance sheet, do you have more money coming in than going out? What are the sources of money coming in? For the money that is going out, is it paying off debts, or is it going towards building assets?

One of my most significant key takeaways when I read the book, was that "wealthy people stack their assets". I only had two assets then, which was a big eye-opener for me, and I wanted to create more.

In chapter five we will meet the "7 Streams of Income" challenge, where you will train your mind to focus on building your first seven streams of income and build the muscle of stacking your asset column. Over 30 days, you will challenge yourself to develop new and creative ways to build your income streams, effectively growing the asset column of your balance sheet. But before we journey there, not all assets are alike. Let's learn the difference between active income and passive income.

Active vs. Passive Income

Active income refers to earnings derived from services you actively perform. Active income could be your salary from a 9-to-5 job, hourly fees from freelance work, or any income that requires your direct and consistent effort. The most significant characteristic of active income is its direct correlation to your time spent working: if you don't work, you don't earn.

In contrast, **passive income** is money earned with little to no ongoing effort on your part. Once you've completed your initial work or investment, income continues without requiring your direct involvement. Examples of passive income include: investment returns, book royalties, rental income from property, dividends from stocks, and earnings from online affiliate marketing. These are just a few examples, but there are hundreds more possiblities today because technology has advanced so much.

Passive income provides freedom. It frees up your time, allowing you to be more strategic about building your asset column or to enjoy more leisure, family time, travel, and pursuit of your other passions. Since you're not trading time for money, it offers financial security, especially if you have multiple passive income streams.

Active income limits your earning potential by your hourly rate and the number of hours you can physically work. Passive income, however, offers scalability. For example, you can sell an online course to ten or ten thousand students with the same initial effort.

Just as diversification in investment reduces risk, having multiple passive income streams can provide a financial safety net. Specific passive income streams, like real estate or dividend-paying stocks, also come with tax advantages. Tax advantages can result in more money in your pocket than an equivalent amount from active income.

Prioritize Passive Over Active Income

Why prioritize passive income over active income? First, prioritizing passive income allows you to break out of the time-effort-earnings cycle and finally decouple how much you earn from how many hours you work. Passive income will enable you to create leverage on your time and to scale your business and operations to make even more passive income.

Second, passive income allows you to build sustainable wealth over time. Passive income, especially when invested wisely, compounds over time. Active income does not. As soon as you stop, it stops. Building passive income streams frees you from chasing your next paycheck.

Finally, well-established passive income sources, like an exitable business (a business you can sell) or real estate, can be passed down through generations, ensuring that your financial legacy supports your loved ones. Choosing to focus on and build passive income streams lets you build legacy and generational wealth for your family for years to come.

Start A Business, Not A Side Hustle

"If you cannot step away from your business for two weeks, then what you have is another job, not a business," Tony Robbins said at Business Mastery, a seminar that I had attended because I was looking to break out of the plateau that I was in at the time.

I felt a pit in my stomach. At the time, I *couldn't* step away from my consulting firm because *I was* my consulting firm. I hadn't started a business at all. I had created a fancy job with much more tax paperwork.

As you begin considering creating your income streams,

I want to make a finer distinction here between **starting a business** (building passive income) instead of starting a *side hustle* (creating another job for yourself).

A side hustle will demand constant attention and add to your workload rather than freeing you from it. Cash flow equals energy flow, so if you need the money to make a breakthrough and starting a freelance side hustle is the way to reach that goal, that's the right decision. But if you have the time to be strategic, start a business. Create something scalable that can run without you and that you can sell.

If you're thinking of starting a business on the side while still holding down your day job, just make sure you're starting a business (not a side hustle). I recommend starting your business on the side while still holding down your day job, especially if you're a first time business founder. Validate that the business is working and that it's what you want to invest your full time energy into before quitting your day job. Don't quit your main source of cash flow until you're certain your new venture will be able to provide the cash flow that you need — because cash flow equals energy flow.

Don't start a side hustle. Start a business that you can automate, grow, and sell.

Work On The Business, Not In The Business

One last insight I'd like to share is the distinction between working *on* the business and not *in* the business.

Think of your business as an end-to-end system. When working on the system, you're working on the business. When you're doing one of the jobs inside the system, you're working "in" the business (creating extra jobs for yourself).

Sometimes, it's easy to get caught up working in the business because we may be passionate about our product and our customer experiences, and we want things done to a high standard, so we might conclude that it's more efficient for us to get the work done ourselves. But this can be a trap because we're not building a business when we step in. We end up becoming a bottleneck that the business has to flow through.

Working on the business means we can stay strategic. Focusing on automation from the very beginning keeps you focused on working on the business. It prevents you from becoming "the worker" and ensures you remain "the orchestrator" guiding your business's growth and evolution.

3

CHATGPT ENTERS THE CHAT

"Business opportunities are like buses, there's always another one coming." — *Richard Branson*

Meet ChatGPT

I remember when ChatGPT first came out. I was at work, in the office, and a group of coworkers excitedly crowded around a computer. They were asking ChatGPT programming questions and were amazed at the accuracy of its answers. "This is going to replace our jobs!"

"Can it write me an email?" I asked. I had it write me an outbound sales email, and the copywriting was pretty good. I quickly realized that I could tweak the prompts and settings and get it to write copy that I could use daily. Immediately, ideas started forming about the types of applications I could build for end-to-end business automation.

The first thing on my list that I wanted to automate was cold outbound emails! It took a couple of months of constantly hearing about AI before I started using it and thinking about it seriously.

A few months later, I led a team at a company AI hackathon to build an end-to-end outbound automation workflow. Our workflow automatically created a sequence of emails customized to the job title and persona of a person who visited certain pages of our website. Seeing how quickly we were able to put this together was eye-opening. I was hooked!

ChatGPT was launched on November 30, 2022, and is the fastest-growing application *ever*. To put things in perspective, ChatGPT reached 100 million monthly active users just two months after its launch, faster than the nine months it took TikTok to get to 100 million users.

OpenAI, the company that launched ChatGPT, was founded in 2015 and launched the first version of GPT-1 in 2018, GPT-2 in 2019, and GPT-3 in 2020 before building up to the viral launch of GPT-4 in 2022.

Despite all the hype and virality, we're still only at the beginning. Only 180 million people use ChatGPT every month; out of the 7.9 billion people worldwide, that's still only 2.28% of the global population. We're only just getting started.

As of the writing of this books' version in January 2024, the current date cutoff for ChatGPT-4 is April 2023. It also has a much longer context window to input longer prompts. The latest model's token context window went from 36,000 to 128,000 tokens (about the number of words for 300 book pages).

What are some of the things you can use ChatGPT for? In the next section, we will cover specific use cases for ChatGPT.

ChatGPT Use Cases for Business, Wealth Generation, and Personal Development

In this section, I will walk through my favorite use cases for ChatGPT for ongoing learning, building businesses, and personal development.

ChatGPT Use Case 1: Personal Tutor

One of my favorite all-time use cases is using ChatGPT as my tutor. You can take advantage of the voice chat feature on iOS and talk directly with it. Unlike Siri and Alexa, it has great voices you can choose from that sound quite pleasant and feel like you're talking to a real person. I especially like to use the voice feature when driving and ask it to teach me about random things that I may be curious about.

Here are a few examples of prompts you can use to have ChatGPT explain concepts to you:

1. *Can you teach me about passive income?*
2. *What are the differences between swell, surf, and surge?*
3. *Can you explain to me in simple terms how serverless functions work?*

Follow your curiosity. Get answers to your questions much faster and ask follow-on questions to understand finer distinctions. Ask it to simplify concepts for you or distinguish between two concepts that seem very similar.

ChatGPT Use Case 2: Ask ChatGPT for feedback on your business, market analysis, strategy, and more

We can iterate and improve our products, services, and businesses with feedback.

Here are some examples of prompts you can use to get feedback on your emails, proposals, and strategies.

Business Plan Feedback Prompt: Here is an initial draft of my business plan. What are some of its strengths and weaknesses? How can I make it better?

Revenue Model Feedback Prompt: Here is how I'm thinking about monetizing my start-up. What are some suggestions for optimizing my pricing and monetization?

Marketing Plan Feedback: I'm presenting this go-to-market plan to my leadership next week. What critical aspects of my plan are missing? What else can I do to make it better?

ChatGPT Use Case 3: Use ChatGPT to brainstorm business, product, and marketing ideas

ChatGPT can be a great brainstorming partner, especially combining intersections of topics that may be more challenging to come up with off the cuff. I like to prompt it to generate a specific number of ideas — maybe five ideas, maybe ten.

You can prompt it to generate lists of ideas and explore different angles or perspectives, simulate scenarios, create analogies, and even combine concepts from unrelated fields.

Passive Income Prompt Ideas
• *What are passive income ideas that I could build with GPT?*
• *What are passive income ideas at the intersection of technology, health, fitness, and meditation that I can build?*

Industry Focused Ideas
• *What are novel startup ideas in the health and wellness industry?*
• *What are innovative startup ideas for AI and Machine Learning?*

Problem Solution Approach
• *Create startup concepts that solve common issues faced by small business owners.*
• *Create startup concepts that solve common issues faced by the growing aging population.*

Emerging Trends
• *What startup ideas leverage the rise of AI and automation?*
• *What are some startup ideas for serving all the AI companies that are getting started?*

ChatGPT Use Case 4: Understand customer challenges & brainstorm solutions

AS STARTUP FOUNDERS or business owners, we can be so focused on perfecting our product that we must remember to stay in touch with our customers. We need to remember their challenges and how important it is to solve them.

How deeply do we understand our customer's challenges? We can use ChatGPT to go one level deeper and to create new product offerings, improvements, and marketing materials that genuinely meet their needs and add value to their lives.

You can ask ChatGPT to understand your customer's challenges better.

1. What are the most common challenges customers in my industry face? What pain points are often associated with this specific customer need?

2. "What are common challenges that a {job title} might encounter while they're {performing action}?

You can also get ahead of your own challenges.

1. What are common challenges I may face while creating passive income?

2. Now that you have a list of challenges, you can ask, "What are some ways that I can get ahead of these challenges?"

Not only can ChatGPT support you with understanding challenges that your customer may be facing so that you can address them with your products and services, but it can also support you with getting ahead of your own challenges, as you build your income streams.

ChatGPT Use Case 5: Visualize Your Success

Visualization is a technique often used by athletes to improve their performance. By creating a vivid and detailed mental image of success, they're better able to perform at that level during game time.

A 1996 study in the "Journal of Sports Sciences" explored

the effect of mental imagery on the performance of basket-ball free throws. This study divided participants into groups, one practicing free throws physically and another using only mental visualization. The results showed that the group practicing with mental imagery improved their free throw performance nearly as much as those who physically practiced.

Why not use ChatGPT to visualize our success in business and wealth generation? By vividly imagining your success as real, you're intensifying your focus on what you want to create and increasing your focus on *what could go right*. Visualization can connect you with your ideal outcome, fuel your motivation, and empower you to activate and take massive action that spurs you further and faster in the direction that you want to go.

Here are some examples that you can use for visualizing massive success building your passive streams of income:

"You are a performance coach specializing in visualization. Guide me through a visualization to help me internalize successfully implementing three passive income businesses with skill and ease. Help me internalize generating abundant wealth and prosperity for me and my family."

"You are a performance coach specializing in visualization. Guide me through a visualization to help me start a company and grow it to a billion-dollar valuation. Help me internalize generating abundant wealth and prosperity for me and my family."

ChatGPT Use Case 6: "The God Prompt"

"Have you heard about The God Prompt?" My friend Ra chirped enthusiastically. We were catching up over the weekend and exchanging our latest ideas about startups, AI, and passive income.

I was skeptical, *mainly* because it was called "The God Prompt"! Begrudgingly, I tried it and was pleasantly surprised at how intelligent it turned out.

The "God Prompt" is a way for you to use ChatGPT to get feedback on your prompts and improve your prompt writing skills.

Here is how it works. First, you will paste in "The God Prompt" into ChatGPT and press enter. Then, submit the prompt you want it to give you feedback on.

Then, ChatGPT will give you feedback on your prompt and how to improve it. It will have a conversation with you, asking how you would like to guide and improve the prompt.

Visit **bit.ly/godprompt** to copy and paste the prompt into ChatGPT.

Here is the prompt:

"I want you to become my Expert Prompt Creator. Your goal is to help me craft the best possible prompt for my needs. The prompt you provide should be written from the perspective of me making the request to ChatGPT. Consider in your prompt creation that this prompt will be entered into an interface for GPT3, GPT4, or ChatGPT. The prompt will include instructions to write the output using my communication style. The process is as follows: 1. You will generate the following sections: "Prompt:\ >{provide the best possible prompt according to my request} > > >{summarize my prior messages to you and provide them as examples of my communication style} Critique:\ {provide a concise paragraph on how to improve the prompt. Be very critical in your response. This section is intended to force constructive criticism even when

*the prompt is acceptable. Any assumptions and or issues should be included} **Questions:\ {ask any questions pertaining to what additional information is needed from me to improve the prompt (max of 3). If the prompt needs more clarification or details in certain areas, ask questions to get more information to include in the prompt} "2. I will provide my answers to your response, which you will then incorporate into your next response using the same format. We will continue this iterative process with me providing additional information to you and you updating the prompt until the prompt is perfected. Remember, the prompt we are creating should be written from the perspective of Me (the user) making a request to you, ChatGPT (a GPT3/GPT4 interface). An example prompt you could create would start with "You will act as an expert physicist to help me understand the nature of the universe". Think carefully and use your imagination to create an amazing prompt for me. Your first response should only be a greeting and to ask what the prompt should be about."*

Visit **bit.ly/godprompt** to copy and paste the prompt into ChatGPT.

ChatGPT Use Case 7: Role Play

Are you practicing for a test, preparing for an interview, or working to refine your sales skills? Or perhaps you need to prepare for an upcoming meeting or negotiation where you may encounter specific questions? Now you can use ChatGPT for role-playing.

Ask ChatGPT to role play for your ideal scenario, give it the parameters that it needs to work with, and you're off to the races.

Here are some prompts to get your role play started:

1. Can you role-play for an upcoming interview with me?

2. Can you role-play a negotiation call with me?

3. I have a meeting coming up with my Head of Sales and CMO to present a GTM Verticalization strategy. I want to ensure my present strategy is precise, specific, actionable, and impactful. Can we role-play that meeting?

Practical Tips: Writing & Syntax for Structuring Prompts

In this section, we're going to dive into practical tips for structuring prompts – the actual syntax of what you will write in ChatGPT. Here are four tips you can follow to become more skillful at prompting.

Practical Tip 1: Be Specific & Include Relevant Details in Your Prompt

One of the first things you may notice when getting started with prompt engineering is "garbage in, garbage out." You get what you ask for. The quality of its answers can mirror the quality of your questions.

To get the most out of ChatGPT, do your best to write clear, structured, and concise prompts.

The more specific you can be, the better your results will be. Whenever possible, include relevant details, helpful context, and be descriptive about the output you're expecting.

For example, you could ask, "What are the benefits of a healthy diet?" A more precise question might be, "What are the benefits of a Mediterranean diet vs a Japanese diet for a 35-year-old woman considering cardiovascular health?"

Specificity allows you to narrow down the scope of your answer, enabling ChatGPT to meet your needs more closely.

As you prompt ChatGPT more, you will naturally find that your initial question may have been too broad, and you'll naturally start writing more specific queries. Over time, regularly prompting ChatGPT may even change your thoughts into more detailed, precise ones.

By being detailed and specific, you minimize guesswork and can get to actionable insights faster.

Practical Tip 2: Separate Content in ChatGPT Using Delimiters

Delimiters act as markers or separators, providing clear boundaries within your prompt to ChatGPT. To enhance clarity, especially in multifaceted tasks, use delimiters like triple quotation marks, XML tags, or section titles.

For instance, if you're asking for a pros and cons analysis followed by a summary, you might instruct ChatGPT to structure its output as follows:

<Pros>...</Pros>
<Cons>...</Cons>
<Summary>...</Summary>

Outlining the structure in your prompt gives the model a clear format to follow, ensuring ChatGPT follows each section systematically.

While ChatGPT is adept at parsing complex language for intricate tasks, it helps to have explicit delimiters. By using delimiters, you streamline the model's processing, ensuring a more precise, more organized, and on-point response. Remember, the easier you make ChatGPT understand your request, the better the outcome.

Practical Tip 3: Specify the Steps Required for a Task

For tasks that follow a logical progression or a structured method, laying out the task in a step-by-step format can be beneficial for getting the exact output that you're expecting.

You could prompt, "Write me a blog post on passive income." But the output of that prompt could be anything.

If you need to follow a specific format, you can define the steps as follows:

You are writing a blog post on the topic of passive income with the following structure:
1. Intro Quote
2. Passive Income Challenges
3. Visualization Intro
4. Visualization Exercise
5. Transition
6. Blog Body
7. Resource Recommendation
8. Outro Quote
9. Call to Action
10. Conclusion

I want you only to write section 1. Intro Quote. In this blog section, identify a quote related to passive income. Use balanced, straightforward language and writing style.

By breaking down your request into a clear sequence, you are providing ChatGPT with a much clearer roadmap to follow that meets your designed structure.

Practical Tip 4: Direct the Model to Adopt a Persona

Directing ChatGPT to assume a specific persona can tailor the tone, style, and content of its response to your needs. Using a system message or explicit instruction at the beginning of your prompt, you can work with a particular expertise you wish the model to embody.

First, you can ask at a high level the different types of personas you can work with depending on what you're trying to do (build a business, identify investments, save for retirement).

> *What are five types of personas that I can have ChatGPT embody to help me build, scale, and grow my business?*

Or, if you already have a specific persona in mind that is relevant to the business and industry you're working with, take the shortcut and get straight to defining them in the prompt.

> *Can you take on the role of an experienced founder and CEO of a billion-dollar software company? I'm scaling a B2B software company. At what stage in ARR or otherwise should I consider beginning verticalization?*

By defining a persona, you're requesting information and feedback through a particular lens, which can make the response more contextually relevant or creatively aligned with your purpose.

Conclusion

I hope you're as excited as I am about all the possibilities we are only beginning to leverage by using ChatGPT daily. Even though there may be a lot of hype, it's important to remember that this is still only the beginning of an incredible opportunity to change how we work. 98% of people still haven't even begun to use ChatGPT! That said, in the examples so far, we've been restricted to *chatting* with ChatGPT via the chat interface. What if we want to use its intelligence and computing power to build custom applications to automate our passive income streams? Head on over to the next chapter where we'll meet our new best friend: Retool.

4

RETOOL TAKES THE STAGE

"Any sufficiently advanced technology is indistinguishable from magic." — *Arthur C. Clarke*

ChatGPT, Meet Retool

One of the key things we learned about in the millionaire mindsets chapter is the importance of **working on the business, not in the business.** Working on the business means automating systems and refining how all the pieces fit together. You want to get to the point where you have automated all the pieces of your business until it can run without you. One of my all-time favorite tools for automating businesses is Retool.

One limitation of only working with the ChatGPT interface is that you're always in the chat box. What if you could access the technology and use it to automate tasks for you in the background? Retool is a way for you to access the GPT-4 APIs to build custom apps and workflows that can take care of the automation for you.

What is Retool? Retool is a platform for building custom business software and workflow automations. You can use it to create custom AI apps to automate your income streams using the GPT-4 API endpoints instead of directly chatting through the interface.

You can connect Retool to OpenAI, Anthropic, Claude, or any custom LLM available through an API, and start building custom AI apps in minutes. One of Retool's key value propositions is speed of development. Without Retool, you would have to code this all from scratch, which can take up a lot of time and be more difficult to maintain. Retool lets you move faster to focus on building your business, not wrangling code. You can quickly create the custom apps you need and stay focused on on optimizing your income streams.

Retool was founded in 2017 in San Francisco, California by David Hsu and Anthony Guo who noticed that every single company has internal tools that are built and maintained by teams of engineers, costing companies millions of dollars. They started Retool to completely transform how all software is made, starting with reducing the complexity of building and maintaining internal tools from scratch, so that teams can stay focused on net new revenue generating features.

I joined Retool in June 2020, inspired by the incredible team, the product they have built, and the traction they had made with the business. Not only was the team some of the most brilliant people I have ever met, but everyone had a "no-ego" way of staying focused and putting in their best work, building the best products, and doing their work impeccably.

Over the last few years, the company has grown from 20 to 300 employees as of this writing and from serving our first 100 customers to over 8000 customers worldwide. Today, the fastest-growing start-ups and leading Fortune 500 enterprises use Retool to power and automate their business.

The product has increased in surface area from focusing on internal tools to enabling developers to build back-end automations, mobile applications, and customer-facing apps.

Do you need to be an engineer to build on Retool? No, you don't need to be an engineer to build on Retool; anyone can get started, and it's easy to learn. If you are an engineer, Retool helps you move 10x faster, up-leveling your productivity and output with excellent developer ergonomics. Even if you know just a little about web development, you can go far in Retool.

In this chapter, I'm excited to show you how you can use Retool to build and automate various AI processes for your business with speed. Let's get started!

Introducing Retool

In this section, I will walk you through how to use Retool, and we will build several simple AI applications together. To support different learning styles, I also made videos of all of these tutorials so that you can watch the video and follow along if that's easier. Visit **https://www.youtube.com/@ adara-js** to watch the video tutorials.

So, let's go ahead and get started! Visit retool.com to create a free account.

When you first create an account and log in, you will be taken to the home screen, where you can see a list of your Apps. In the navigation bar, you will also see the option to navigate across your Apps, Resources, Database, Query Library, and Workflows.

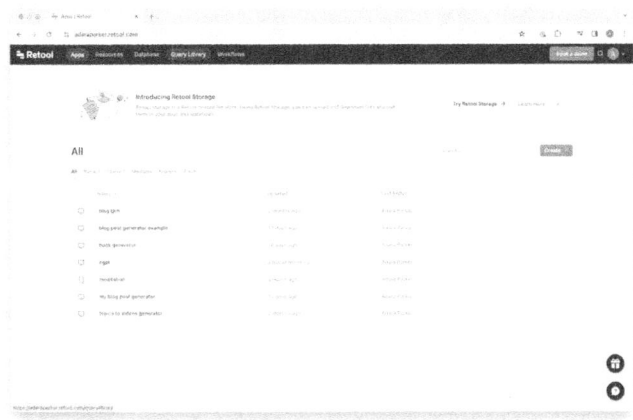

Retool home screen where you can see all your apps

But before going into creating an app, we're going to click on the Resources tab, where you can see all the Resources that you can bring into your Retool apps. In Retool lingo, a "resource" is any data source; it can be a database, API, third-party software, and AI LLMs like OpenAI, Anthropic, Cohere, and more.

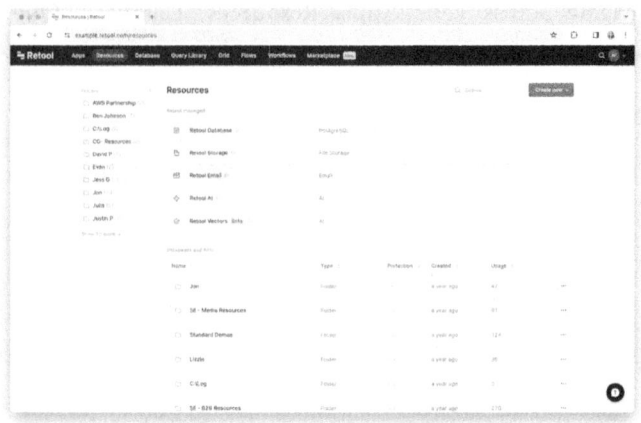

Resources tab where you can see all your data sources

Inside the resources tab, you can see Retool Managed Resources at the top, which are all the Retool back-end products that help you spin up a database with ease.

In the bottom half, you'll be able to see all the resources that you own and manage that you've connected to your Retool instance.

To take a look at what we can connect to our instance, let's click the blue Create New button in the upper right-hand corner.

For now, notice the Retool AI resource as well, which we will get to a little bit later in the chapter.

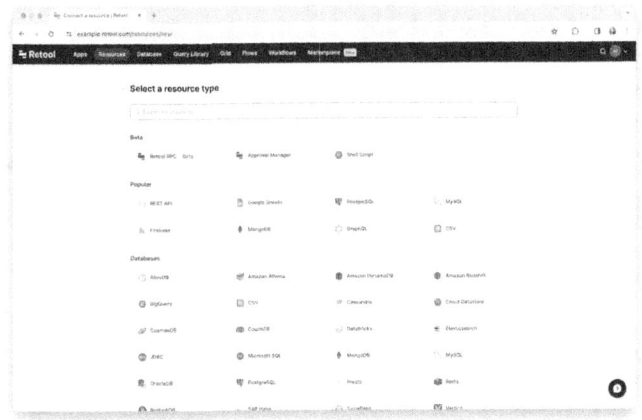

A list of all the resources we can connect into Retool

You can connect any major database (Postgres, MySQL, MongoDB, Oracle, SAP) as well as any REST API, GraphQL API, and gRPC into Retool so that you can build custom logic on top of all of your APIs, data sources, and more.

Now that you've gotten a little bit of a tour, let's go ahead and create our first Retool app. In this example, we're going to be using AI to automate content generation for our business.

Intro to Building Our First AI App on Retool

Let's say that you've decided to start a blog as one of your passive streams of income. To automate your business, you've decided to build a Retool app that generates blog posts for you based on topics that you give it. First, we're going to build a simple version of this together to show you how you can build end-to-end apps in Retool. And then, we're going to automate it, complicate it, and customize it to our needs.

Step 1: Create a blank app

Go ahead and create a blank app, which drops you right into editor mode, where you can see a blank canvas on which to build your interface and navigation panels on the left and right of the screen.

Our app as a blank canvas

On the top left-hand corner, we're going to click the "+" icon and pop open the **Components Panel**.

The Components Panel shows us all the pre-built components that we can drag and drop onto the canvas to create our app's front-end interface. Components include things like text input fields, tables, buttons, and charts. If you think about it, every business software tool is going to be made up of the same building blocks. You'll usually see tables, text input fields, charts, and buttons. Having pre-made components is going to save you a lot of time.

Components panel

Let's go ahead and create a simple interface on the canvas, which will consist of a Text Component, a Text Input Field, a Text Area, and a Button.

Drag and drop the components onto the canvas to look something like this:

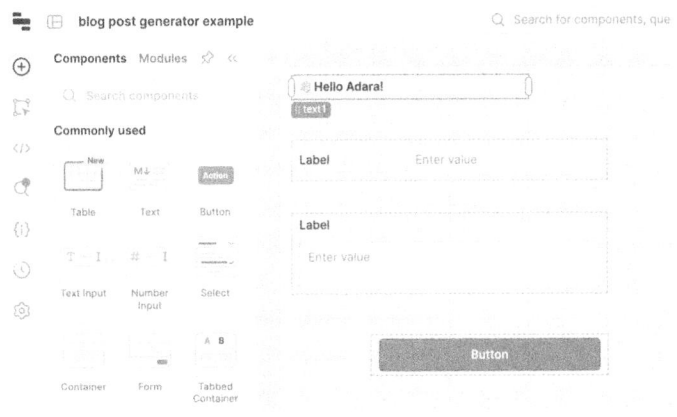

Our blog post generator interface

On your screen, it should say "Hello {Your Name}"

instead of mine. Let's go ahead and click on the text component and change that.

When you click on the text component, you'll notice that the component configuration panel will appear on the right-hand side. You will be able to modify any component's properties from this panel.

Component configuration panel

Let's zoom in on the Value Property of the text component.

Text component Value property

See where it says Hello {{ current_user.firstName || 'friend' }}? This is where we can configure what this component will show. Here, we can see that we're writing some markdown and utilizing what we call *double curly braces*.

Everything in between the double curly braces {{ }} is where you can write code. This code will get interpreted to java-script and is what lets you customize the app completely. For now, we're going to delete everything in the box and just type ### Blog Post Generator so that our app has a title.

Now let's click the second component, the *textinput* component. On the right-hand panel, click on "Label" so that we can change the default "Label" to "Topic" because this is where we'll be pasting the topic that we want GPT-4 to create a blog post about.

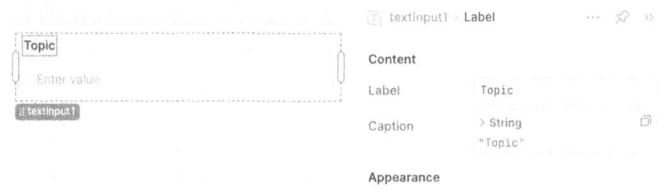

Text input component label

We will do the same for the text area component, where we want to change "Label" to "Blog Post" because this is where we will have gpt output the blog post for us.

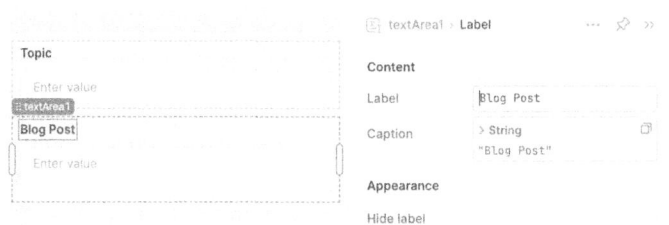

Text input component label

Finally, let's click on the button and update the text on the button to "Create Blog Post".

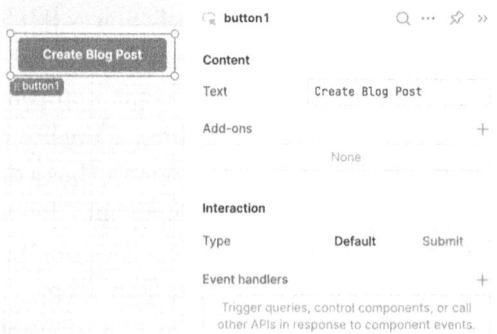

Create blog post button

Now, we're done with the front-end of our app! Your interface should look something like this.

Our updated blog post generator app interface

Now for the fun part: it's time to have the app start interacting with GPT. To have the app start interacting with GPT, click on the </> icon on the lefthand panel under the Components Panel to pull up the Query Builder. This will open up another panel on the left hand side, which is where we can write queries to our data sources (all the databases, APIs, and AI LLMs).

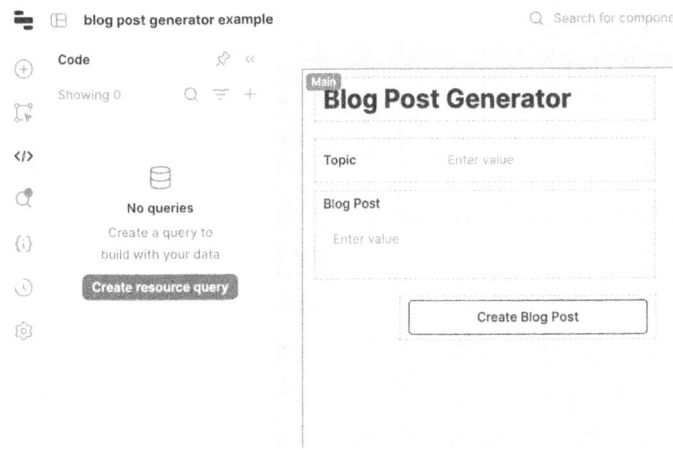

Opening the Code panel on the left

Queries let your components read and write from various data sources and APIs. A query is how we're going to prompt GPT-4. When you write a query, you can use it throughout your application. Your components can "call" a query and cause it to run. For example, a button click can cause your AI query to run. Queries are how you can read and write to and from the various sources of data you'd wish to integrate into your app.

Let's take a brief look at the types of queries we can write. Once the query builder is open, click on the + button to create a new query. There are three types of queries you can write: Resource Queries, Javascript, and Workflows.

Resource Queries: Resource queries are standard CRUD (create, read, update, delete) operations on top of all your databases, APIs, and third-party integrations. An **AI Action** is a type of resource query because we're querying our AI resource.

Javascript: Javascript queries are pure javascript that you can write and call throughout your apps for any kind of custom operations.

Workflows: Workflows are back-end automations that you can call from your applications.

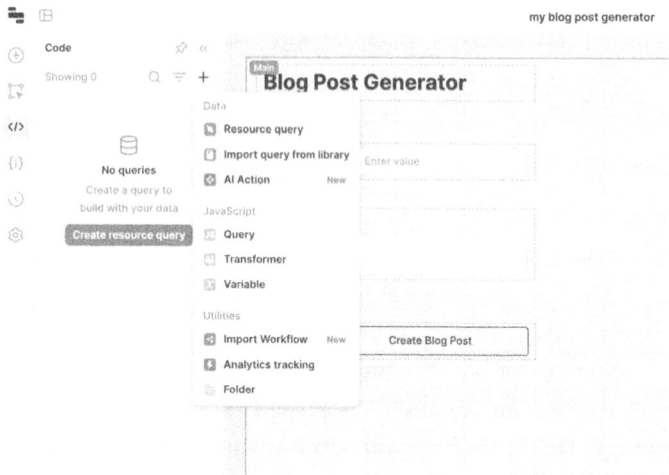

Types of queries

Let's go ahead and write our first AI query by selecting the **AI Action** option from the new query panel.

Writing our first AI query

Here, we can see a detailed view of all the options we can use to configure our AI query. We can specify the Action we want the AI to take and define our prompt in the Input property. We can also configure the system message, temperature, vectors, and models.

AI query settings

If we select the **Action** dropdown, we can see all the types of actions that we can run via GPT-4.

Here is a complete list of all the actions you can run:

Text Actions
Generate text
Summarize text
Classify text

Extract entity from text

Chat

Generate chat response

Document

Convert document to text

Image

Generate image

Generate text from image

Caption image

Classify image

Extract entity from image

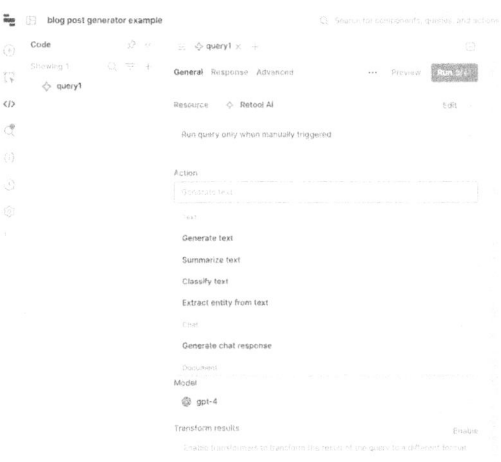

Selecting "Generate text" for our AI query

As you can see, there are many exciting possibilities for building end-to-end apps, considering all of the actions we can take.

Since we're building a blog post generator, let's select Generate Text.

Click on the Input section and enter your prompt. Let's write, "Write me a short blog post about {{textInput1.value}}" where *textInput1* is the name of the text input component and where "value" references the text that we have typed into that component. Let's save our query.

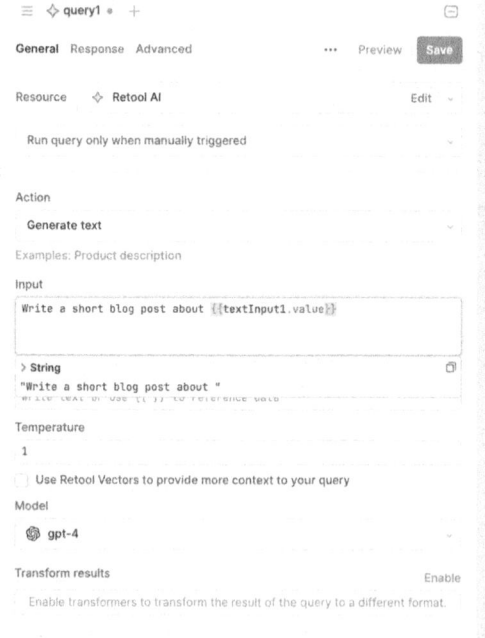

Adding our prompt to the Input section of our AI query

Now that our components are all on the canvas and our query is complete let's wire up the query to the button and its outputs to the text area.

To wire up the output of the query to the text area, click on the Text Area component. On the right-hand side, the component detail view panel will pop up. Let's click on the

Default Value property and use our double curly braces to write {{query1.data}} so that the output of our query (currently called *query1*) will be displayed here after GPT-4 runs.

Connecting our text input's value property to {{query1.data}}

Last but not least, let's click on our "Create Blog Post" button and connect it to our query. After clicking the button, click on "Event Handlers" on the right-hand side. Set the Action to "Control query," and the query we want to fire off is called *query1*. That's it!

Adding an event click handler to our button to run our query

Now, go ahead and exit the builder mode by clicking the play button on the upper right-hand side. Now, we are

in *end-user mode,* which is how you interact with the apps
when you're not actively building them.

Let's go ahead and run the app, asking GPT to write us a
blog post about meditation.

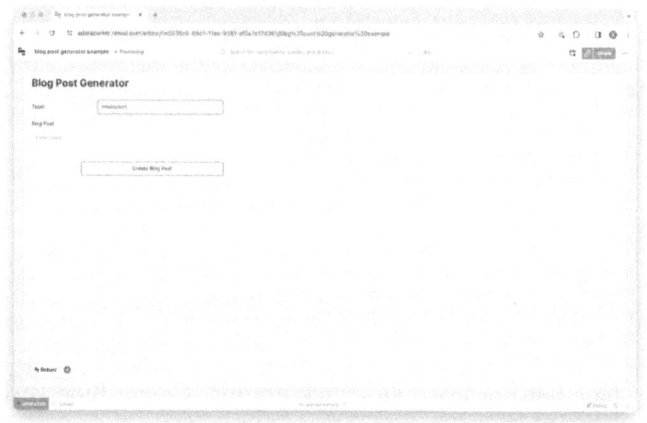

Running our blog post generator with "meditation" as a topic

And that's it! In just moments, we should see our blog
post about meditation. Yay!

Our blog post generator app showing a complete blog post

I hope this simple introduction shows you the exciting app-building capabilities of the platform. You should be able to comfortably navigate components, write simple AI queries, and connect the pieces of an app together using double curly braces.

That said, this is just a simple example, and it still requires us to click a button to generate a blog post, which is honestly not too different from going to ChatGPT and asking it to write us a blog post on meditation.

This takes us to **Retool Workflows**. What if you were able to have Retool and GPT write your blog posts while you sleep? What if you were able to feed it a dozen topics at a time and have it loop through and write blog posts on each one so that you had your entire blog written for you automatically?

Let's walk through how to do that in the next section on Retool Workflows.

Intro to Retool Workflows

Retool Workflows is the automation layer of the Retool platform. Workflows gives you a set of building blocks that you can chain together to model any complex process. Workflows let you define steps that run in the background, either on a regular interval, via webhooks, or when we explicitly call the workflow to run from an app.

In this example, we're going to use workflows to generate blog posts automatically for us.

Let's get started. Navigate to the Workflows tab from our main navigation bar. Here, we can see all our workflows, usage analytics, as well as folders to store and organize our workflows.

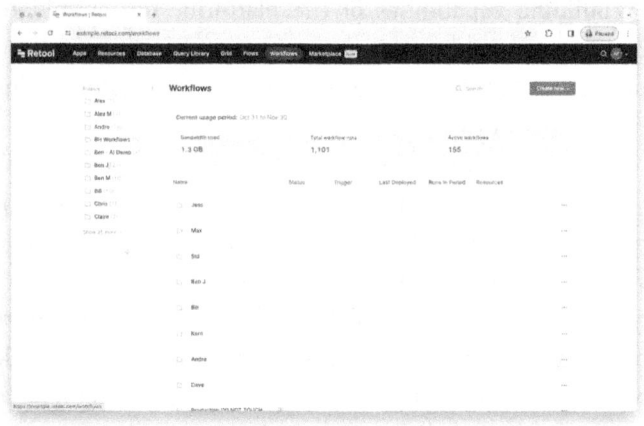

Retool Workflows Tab

Let's create a new workflow by clicking the blue "Create New" button in the upper right-hand corner.

We'll be taken to our workflows canvas, where we can

see an example workflow with a *start trigger block* and a *code block.*

Retool Workflows Canvas

If we go ahead and run this template workflow by clicking the "Run" button with the play icon in the upper right-hand corner, the start trigger will fire and execute the code in the code block.

Viewing the run history panel from the bottom

The Run History panel will pop up from the bottom, and you'll be able to see that a workflow run has occurred with detailed logs that let you inspect the output of each block.

In this example, the code block ran and returned the "hello world" message from the code block that we were expecting.

Great, so let's say that we want to build a workflow to automate writing a blog post for us on any topic. Let's say that we have three prompts that run in sequence and a block that adds the output of the prompts together.

First, let's take a look at the *startTrigger* block. This is the block that fires off the workflow. When we click on it, the startTrigger configuration panel opens up on the left, and we can see that we can either configure it to fire off on a webhook call or on a regular schedule. For our blog generator, we're going to be calling it from our app by feeding it a list of topics, so we're going to configure it to fire off on a webhook call. All we have to do is turn on the webhook toggle.

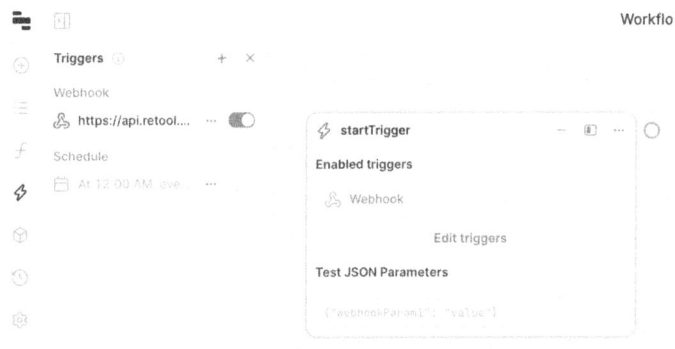

Close-up view of our startTrigger block

Looking more closely at the startTrigger block, you'll notice that we enabled the webhook trigger and that the remaining item left to define is the input parameter. This is where we're going to feed our blog post topics. The start-Trigger block is going to expect this input in JSON format.

Let's create our input parameter as {"topic": "value"}. When we actually call this workflow, we're going to replace "value" with any topic we want, and it will pass that value into the workflow block. Your startTrigger block should look like this.

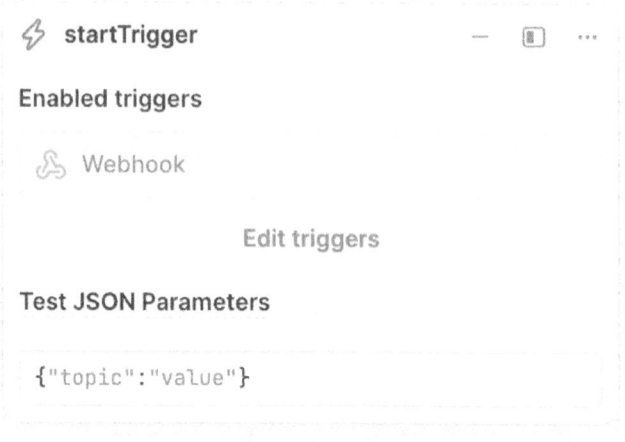

Adding JSON parameter structure to our startTrigger block

Now that that's set up, we're going to delete the code block and click the circle in the upper right-hand corner of the startTrigger block to take a look at all the types of blocks we can call after our startTrigger.

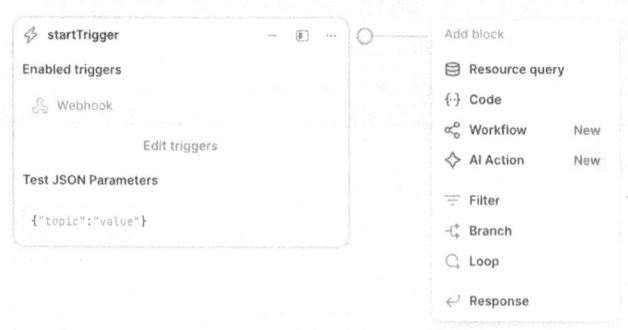

Connecting our startTrigger block to a new block type

Resource Block Types:

Resource Query: These are queries to and from our databases, APIs, and third-party libraries

Code Blocks: Here, we can write custom code in javascript and python

Workflow Block: This block will call another workflow

AI Action: This block lets us call our LLM APIs

Functions: Define & reuse queries and logic

Logic Block Types:

Filter: Filter results based on defined conditions

Branch: Perform different actions depending on conditions

Loop: Iterate through data sets

Response: Return our response

GREAT, now that we have a sense of the different types of blocks that we can use to build our workflow, let's select *AI Action* block.

Connecting our startTrigger block to an AI block

In the input text let's paste our first prompt, which is "Share a quote about {{startTrigger.data.topic}}". Here {{startTrigger.data.topic}} is how we are referencing the topic that's being passed into the workflow. We're referencing the startTrigger block and then we're accessing its data property and finally selecting the topic (which we defined as an input property in the beginning of the tutorial).

Let's test that the AI block is working as expected by clicking the run icon in the upper right hand corner. We can see it works as expected because it generated a response in its own data property at the bottom of the workflow block.

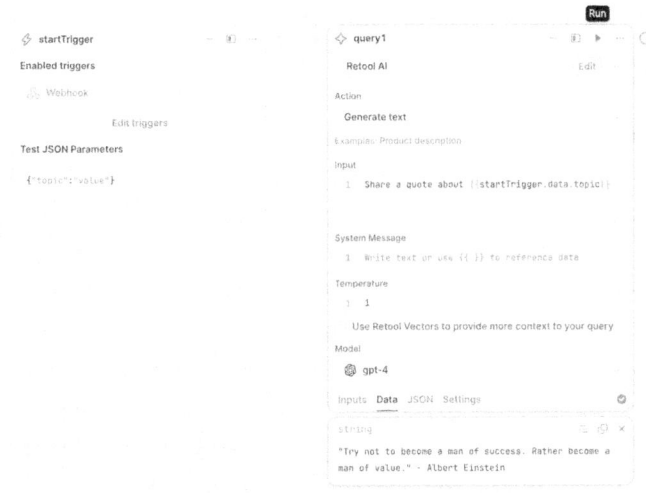

Filling out and running the AI block

We can see that it's working as expected because it generated a quote, which is great!

Let's go ahead and create the second workflow AI block by clicking the green circle in the upper right-hand corner of the first AI block.

Connecting a second AI block

Let's give it the following prompt, "Write the first part of a blog post about common challenges that people may face when getting started with this topic: {{startTrigger.data.topic}}.

Finally, let's create the third block, and this time, we're going to have it reference the data output of the second block so that it knows what it generated before and can continue generating relevant content.

Instead of "Generate text," we're going to select the "Generate Chat Response" Action. Notice that doing so changes the properties of this block accordingly. Since this is a chat response action, we now have the ability to reference the *Message History* so that it has the right context in memory. In this case, we want to reference the initial part of the blog post that was generated in query 2.

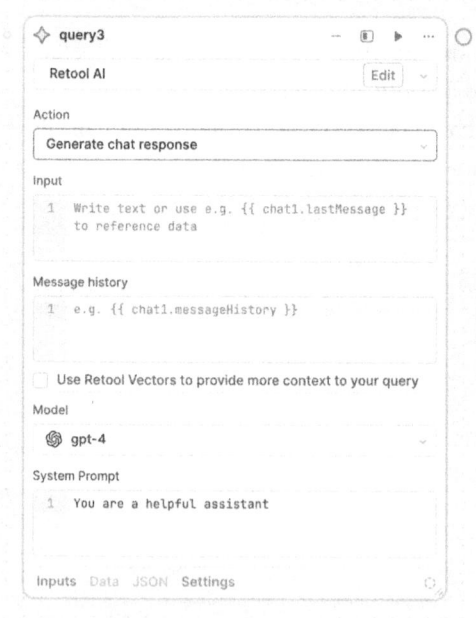

Using the "Generate chat response" action in our AI block

To do this, first, we'll prompt, "Write the final part of a blog post offering solutions on how to overcome common challenges that people may face when getting started with this topic: {{startTrigger.data.topic}}."

In the Message History, we're going to reference the previous block by giving it an array where the content is the output of the previous block. Here, we want it to be able to reference the previous block.

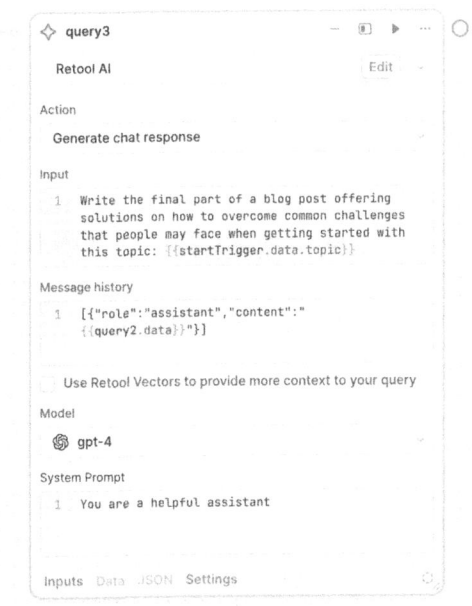

Referencing Message History in our Chat Response block

And that's it! Let's go ahead and run the third block as well to make sure the prompts are generating the output that we would expect.

Your workflow should look something like this:

Our workflow so far

Now, we're going to stitch everything together with a code block and some simple javascript.

Your code block will look something like this, and when you test it, you should see all the content from the previous blocks stitched together.

Close up view of our code block

Now for the final step: what if you wanted to have this blog post stored in a database for referencing later? What if you also wanted to get an email every time the blog post was done and ready for review?

You can also set up both in parallel with Retool. Let's finish the example!

Click the green dot in the upper right-hand of the code block, and first, let's create a Resource Query. We're going to select Retool Database.

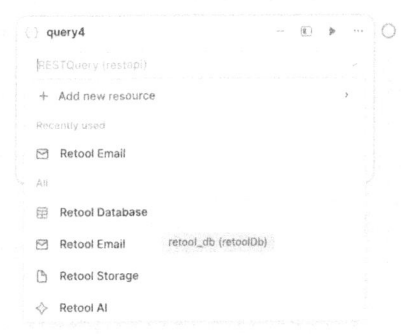

Selecting Retool Database

When we select it, we're going to be able to see all the tables that we have access to in our database.

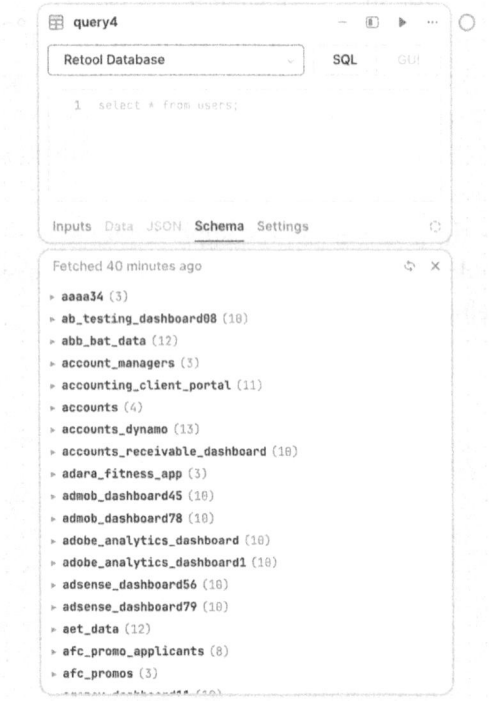

Detail view of all the tables in our Retool Database

We don't have a table for our blog posts yet, so let's create one. In a new tab, open up your Retool instance home page and click the Database link in the upper main navigation bar.

Select "Database" in the navigation bar

Here, we can see all the tables in our database. Let's create a new table called *blog_posts* by clicking the "+" button in the very right-hand corner.

Our Retool Database

Our new table will have two fields, *blog_content*, and *created_at* (so that we can keep track of when they were created). Over time, we can add and modify these.

Here is our *blog_content* text field.

Creating the schema of our Retool Database

Let's make a *created_at* text field as well and select Field Type as "created time". And that's it!

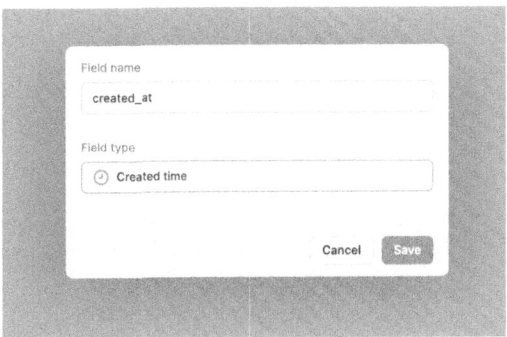

Creating the schema of our Retool Database

Your Retool Database blog_posts table should look like this.

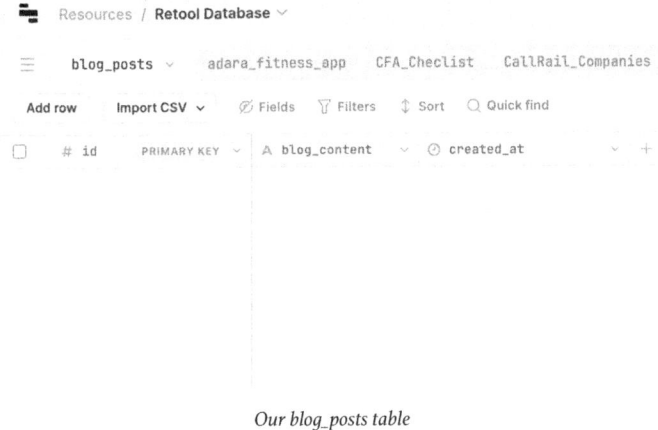

Our blog_posts table

Now, let's go back to your workflow block and have it post your blog posts to the database table upon completion.

In the workflow block, toggle GUI mode. The interface will change to assist you with reading and writing to your tables so that you can save time by not having to write raw SQL.

Inserting our blog post into our blog_posts table

Now, let's fill out the block as follows. Let's select the blog_posts table. Let's configure our action type to insert a record.

And then, in the changeset, all we have to do is set blog_-content to {{code1.data}}, and you'll see if you hover your mouse over the double curly braces that you can preview the data that will be written to your database.

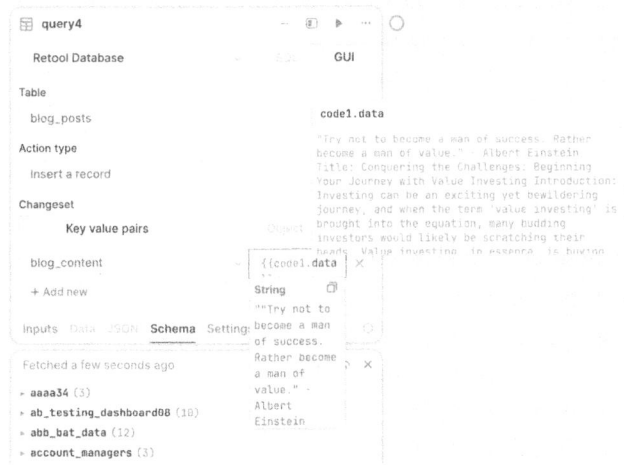

Clicking play to make sure our query4 block works as expected

Go ahead and click "play" in the upper right-hand corner of query4 to run. Then, if you pop over to your Retool Database, you should see your blog.

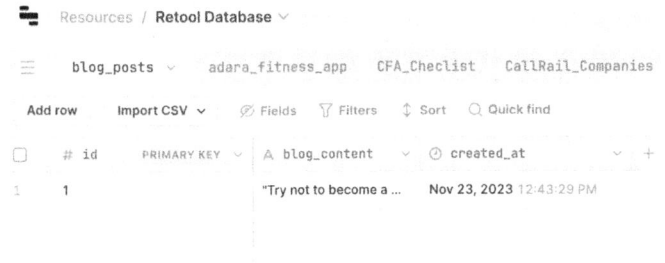

Seeing our blog post updated in our blog_posts table

The last thing to set up is an email notification to let you know when the blog post is ready to review.

Let's click the small circle in the upper right-hand corner

of our code block and create a second resource block. These two will fire off at the same time.

Connecting a second simultaneous block

Let's select the "Retool Email" resource.

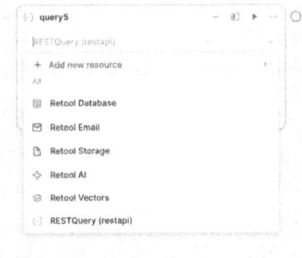

Selecting Retool Email as a resource

Write your email in the to: field. In the body of the email, write {{code1.data}} so that you can start reading the blog post from your email upon completion.

Filling out the details of our email

Feel free to click the run button to give it a try. Always a delight to see the email notification hit my inbox!

Your blog post is ready!   ⟲ ⏱ ✉

Challenges and solutions for value investing beginners

noreply@example.retool-email.com   12:47 PM

"Try not to become a man of success. Rather become a man of value." - Albert Einstein

Title: Conquering the Challenges: Beginning Your Journey with Value Investing

Introduction:

Investing can be an exciting yet bewildering journey, and when the term 'value investing' is brought into the equation, many budding investors would likely be scratching their heads. Value investing, in essence, is buying stocks for less than their intrinsic value or worth. It is a strategy that requires savvy, patience, and tenacity for one to reap considerable returns in the long run.

However, for those embarking on this journey, several challenges commonly arise that may seem daunting. Understanding these challenges is the first step to navigating the world of value investing effectively. This blog post aims to break down these challenges, provide a framework to comprehend them, and set the groundwork for a fruitful journey into the world of value investing.

Challenge #1: Understanding the Concepts

One of the more common challenges in starting with value investing is understanding the terms, concepts, and jargon used in the realm of investing. Concepts such as intrinsic value, discounted cash flows, or price-to-earnings (P/E) ratios might seem unfamiliar and intimidating for beginners. There's a great deal to master in this respect, which can be overwhelming for those just starting.

Challenge #2: Developing a Value Investor's Philosophy

Simply understanding the basic terms is not enough. You need to digest these concepts fully, crunch numbers, and develop a discerning eye to recognize undervalued stocks that promise good returns. Beginning investors may feel unsure or lack the confidence to make decisions regarding promising and undervalued stocks.

View of the emails in our inbox

Great, now our workflow automation piece is done! If we zoom out and toggle to "tree view" we can easily see the logic we have created.

High level view of our blog post generator workflow so far

Let's deploy our workflow by clicking the Deploy button in the upper right-hand corner. This publishes your workflow live, and then you can call it from your apps. If you have a time-based recurring trigger, it will start running on the schedule that you have determined.

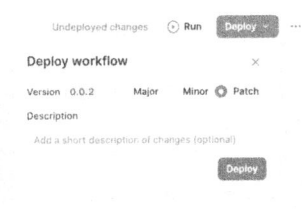

Deploying our workflow

We're in the final stretch! Let's head back to our blog post generator app and update it slightly so that 1) we can feed it a large number of topics and 2) it will fire off this workflow, creating a blog post about each topic.

If we take a look at our original blog post generator app, we'll need to make a few modifications so that we can feed it a number of topics, and it will automatically fire off the workflow to create blog posts on those topics.

Modify the UI as follows:

Updating our UI to automatically generate blog posts via workflow

Let's create a new query, and this time, select "Import Workflow" so that we can call the workflow from the app.

Under the Select Workflow section, let's select the **blog workflow** that we worked on together. In the Workflow Parameters section, we'll want to specify the topic and the value that we want to pass through.

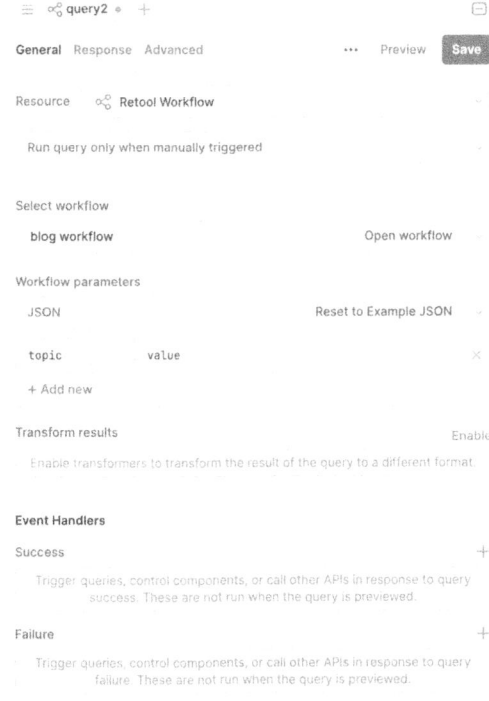

Adding a new query to fire off the workflow from our app

Now, what we'll want to do is write a query that takes all the topics that we put into the text field, loops through them, and then passes them one by one into the workflow.

To do this, we're going to write a javascript query. In this query, I'm going to take my array of topics and iterate through them, passing each one into the workflow by calling query2.

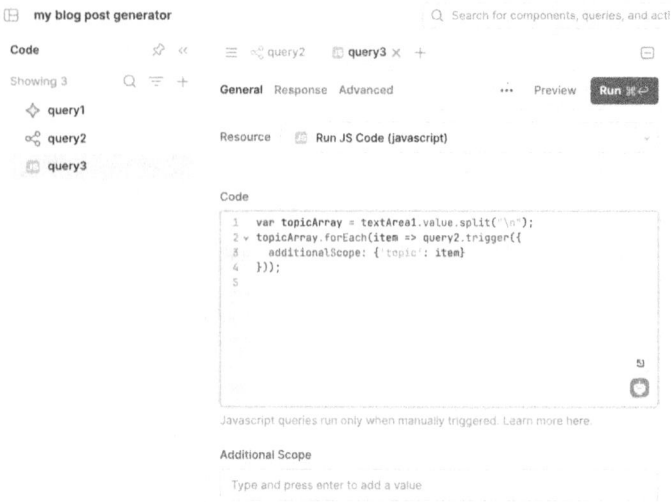

Javascript that loops through the topics and passes them into our workflow

To make sure that our workflow knows to expect the dynamic topics, we're going to make a slight adjustment in the workflow parameters by taking value and using double curly braces here and typing {{topic}} so that it can receive these topics dynamically from our javascript query.

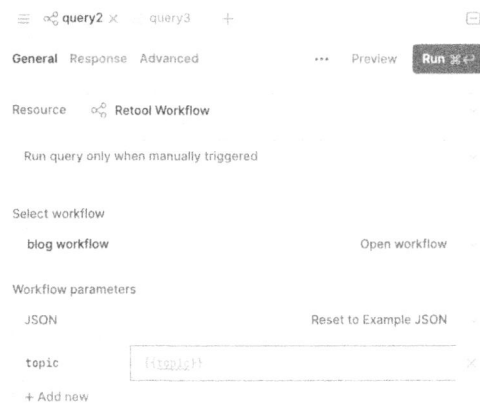

Connecting our topics into the workflow

Last but not least, let's connect our javascript query to our button, type in some topics, and give it a test run!

In end-user mode, let's feed our app some topics like mindfulness, meditation, and stress relief and click "Write Blog Posts".

Submitting multiple topics

When I pop over to my workflow and take a look at the logs, I can see that my three topics are running. For each topic, I can even click on the startTrigger block in the logs and see which one was passed into the workflow to make sure everything looks as expected.

Confirming the workflows are running as expected

So far, so good. After the workflows finish running, you can check your emails and see them all in the thread.

Horray! We can see our blog posts in our email

And there you have it! We just built a blog post generator that can automatically write blog posts for us on any topic while we're stepping away from the computer and email us when they're ready to be reviewed.

Now, you have the basic tools and skills in place to begin using AI and Retool to automate blog posts while you sleep.

We are on our way! But if you actually read the blog posts, they still sound like ChatGPT. What if we want to write blog posts about highly specific topics with internal information that GPT doesn't have access to? Let's get to know Retool Vectors.

Intro to Retool Vectors

Retool Vectors is a managed vector database that enables you to store unstructured text from documents and web pages for use with AI models throughout your Retool applications.

Retool abstracts away the complexities of managing vector databases from scratch and automatically prepares your data for AI models to use and reference.

Let's say that I've already written blog posts and want to start automating blog post generation — but I want new blog posts to still sound like me and to reference things that I've written about before. I can use Retool Vectors to *vectorize* all my blog posts and then *reference* them in our AI blocks so that GPT-4 not only knows what I know but also sounds like me. Here are some use cases for Retool Vectors.

Enterprise Search

A lot of companies have internal knowledge bases that live across many data sources like Confluence, Google Docs, Slack Channels, and more. It can be challenging to find the right information. Do you search Confluence? Or start with Google Docs? Or go straight to asking in a shared Slack channel? With Retool Vectors, you can vectorize all of your company's relevant data and then build a very simple Retool app on top of that data so that you can search and find what you need. A solution like this would mean you no longer have to search a million places to find what you're looking for. You can even create specialized vectors for different teams. For example, the sales and marketing teams may want to reference customer stories and case studies readily, whereas the customer support team may want to reference more technical information specific to the product. These teams' vectors can live in different places, and you can build custom apps and workflows on top of them.

Customer Support Chat Bot

What if you were able to re-use your company's internal documentation, community channels, and previous customer support threads in order to train a customer support bot that helps make your agents perform their jobs with more speed and ease? Retool Vectors can help you vectorize your docs, community channels, and previous customer support threads to feed into the knowledge base of your customer support bot. The bot can start to triage the ticket coming in and offer an outline of an answer for your support agent to increase their productivity. The agent can also chat with the bot to get quicker answers to their questions with respect to debugging a customer issue.

Outbound & Email Copywriting Automation

What if you wanted to AI generate a personalized email to new customers signing up for your product that was specific to their company industry and job function? Maybe in your email, you will start to suggest use cases for your product that are highly relevant to them to expedite activation and shorten sales cycles. You can build this by vectorizing your company's sales data, marketing data, blog posts, and persona information, and then building a Retool workflow which takes the new customer's information upon sign-up, fires off a workflow to draft an intro email given relevant customer data, and then pings a business development rep to reach out given a pre-written email that they can customize. This type of use case can create incredible leverage across your teams by saving your team time from copywriting and by creating a delightful customer experience.

Blog Post Generation

Let's go back to our blog post generator app. Let's say that we're using our blog post generator to write a series of blog posts, but we want it to model our writing style and to have specific knowledge about our industry, blog post topic, and previous content that we've written. With Retool Vectors, we can vectorize our prior written work, social media posts, and industry-specific knowledge and documentation using and then feed that vector into GPT-4 to reference the material.

Retool Vectors is really easy to set up. To start generating vectors, navigate to your Resources Tab and then select Retool Vectors.

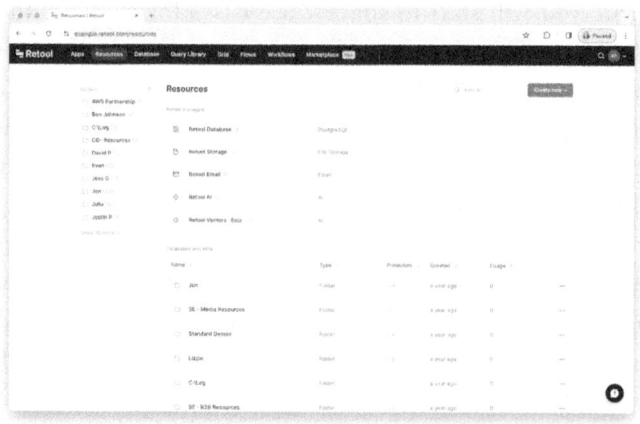

Select "Retool Vectors" from the Resources Tab

Then, select Create Vector in the upper right-hand corner. From here, you will be able to upload a PDF, paste plain text, or paste a URL, which Retool will crawl to extract and vectorize the text.

Creating a Retool Vector

Let's say that we want to write blog posts about trending

health topics. I have paid access to a service called Exploding Topics that gives me insight and data into trending health topics as they start trending. I used Retool's Site URL to crawl through the Exploding Topics site and pull relevant trending health topics to reference in a vector.

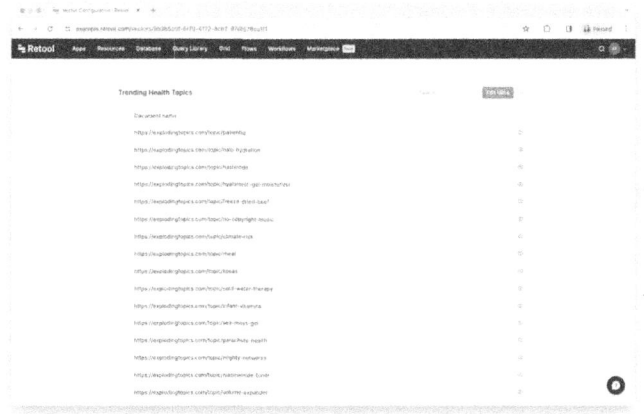

Viewing all the text that has been vectorized

Great! Now that we've vectorized some of the top trending health topics let's create a new app just to test that our content has been vectorized as expected.

Go ahead and drag a chat component onto the canvas and connect it to an AI query. In our AI query, let's click on the checkbox "Use Retool Vectors to provide more context to your query" and select "Trending Health Topics."

And that's it. Once the chat_query1 is saved, it's automatically connected to the chat component. Let's ask it a question specific to the data that we just vectorized to test that it's working.

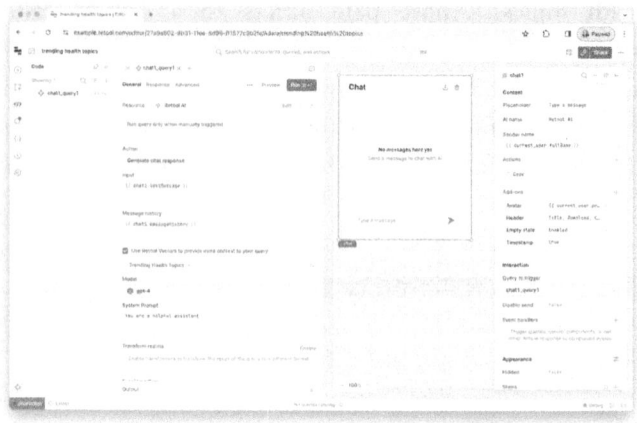

Connecting our Retool Vector to our Chat Component

Let's ask, "Can you tell me about the top 3 trending health topics?"

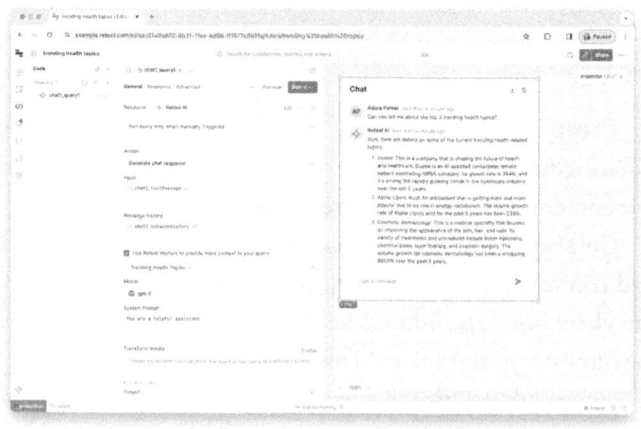

Querying our vectors via the Chat Component

Great, looks like it's querying the vector as expected! Now, we can use this vector in any of the AI queries throughout all of our Retool apps. In every workflow block, you'll see the option to use Retool Vectors as well.

To reference a vector from a workflow block, simply select the check box "Use Retool Vectors to provide more context to your query" and select the relevant vectors you would like to reference.

Referencing a vector from a workflow block

I will leave this to you as homework, but if you want to vectorize specific information you would like your blog post to access, you can add it to Retool Vectors and then select the "Use Retool Vectors" checkbox to reference that in all your AI queries.

Conclusion

We covered a lot of ground in this chapter! We got to meet and explore Retool, build our own blog post generator, automate blog post generation with a workflow, and even vectorize content and use it throughout our AI queries.

Now, you have the basic building blocks to build any AI-powered automation that you can imagine for your business. What if we wanted to automate image generation alongside our blog posts? What if we wanted to automate keyword research followed by blog post generation? What if we wanted to extract text from documents and perform analysis? The possibilities are endless.

I hope you can see how easy, powerful, and delightful it is to build these types of AI automations on the Retool platform. If this really piqued your curiosity, I encourage you to visit my YouTube channel, where I walk through more app-building tutorials and discuss fun and impactful use-case ideas.

Now that we have a good technical base for using ChatGPT and building AI-powered applications, in the next phase of the book, we're going to explore different types of income streams that you can build and automate with AI to build your seven streams of income.

5

THE 7 STREAMS OF INCOME CHALLENGE

"It's not about how much money you make, but how much money you keep, how hard it works for you, and how many generations you keep it for." — *Robert Kiyosaki*

The Average Millionaire Has 7 Streams of Income

"Did you know the average millionaire has at least seven streams of income?" My friend Nidhi said to me one day.

That number was encouraging and auspicious.

"How did it come to be 7?" I asked.

"The number may not be precisely seven, but it's *a lot*. Maybe 7 is a number that catches people's attention."

A lightbulb went off in my head. I just read Rich Dad Poor Dad and was enlightened by the concept of stacking your asset column.

"How many income streams do I have?" I wondered.

I only had two at the time: my business and savings account.

I need to make a solid effort to build up to 7! That's when things clicked.

I wanted to build my asset column, but I needed to make more progress with a specific goal in mind. Having a tangible number like 7 was a helpful goal for getting started. I started imagining seven income streams and was excited about what that could look like. Would I be someone who owned multiple businesses? Would I be more of an investor? What type of business owner or investor would I want to be? How big would I want each of those businesses to be?

I decided then and there to challenge myself and start building my seven income streams as fast as possible. I considered a stream of income any form of cash flow or asset.

I needed to build these out as fast as possible, even if some would begin as tiny investments.

When I got home that evening, I started researching the concept of "seven streams of income." I read through countless personal finance blogs that emphasized the idea until I finally stumbled upon what seemed to be the source of this information.

Tom Corley, the author of "Rich Habits: The Daily Success Habits of Wealthy Individuals," conducted a five-year study examining individuals' habits and financial practices across income brackets. His research revealed an interesting disparity in how affluent individuals approached income generation: a significant percentage of the wealthy participants did not rely on a single income source.

Corley's study did not explicitly mandate the number seven but pointed to the recurring trend of building a portfolio of diverse revenue streams (assets) among the successful.

A few days later, I was catching up with another friend, Kenjin, who had recently attended one of Tony Robbins' Wealth Mastery seminars. He had been saving money and wanting to participate in this seminar for a long time. From what I recall, it was a significant investment to follow, and in this seminar, they would have some of the wealthiest people and best wealth managers in the world teaching you about wealth building and financial freedom.

"Was there anything you learned that surprised you?" I asked eagerly. "Tell me all the secrets!"

"One thing that surprised me," Kenjin said, "was that wealth managers manage their client's portfolios until they have over 13 or more income streams".

But for some reason, my friend seemed a bit discouraged.

"13?! Wow, that's a lot more than I expected. What did you think about it?"

"I don't even know how to create 13 different income streams; it feels too much."

I also noticed that although 13 is an abundant number of income streams, it feels less approachable. I decided there may be no "final number" to get to. The upper bound is endless.

Nevertheless, this validated my mission to build and stack up as many revenue streams as possible to reach my goals.

I re-committed to my own personal seven streams of income challenge and decided that seven would be my correct number. I could always increase it as I grew.

Your 7 Streams of Income Challenge

I invite you to partake in your version of the 7 Streams of Income challenge, where you build your portfolio of 7 income streams, assets, businesses, or cash flow in 30 days.

Why 30 days? Because 30 days is enough for you to take massive action and short enough to have a meaningful sense of urgency.

What would it take for you to identify and build out your seven income streams in 30 days?

The Challenge

In this challenge, there are three steps.

Step 1: Explore all the different income streams that could fit you well.

Step 2: Reflect on which resonates with you and write them down.

Step 3: Commit to which income streams you will build in the next 30 days and take massive action to go "from 0 to 1" for all those income streams.

Ready? Let's begin!

Step 1. Exploring all your possibilities

Exploration is the essence of the human spirit. — Frank Borman

In this section, let's explore all the different types of income you can generate, businesses you can start, and investment opportunities you can consider.

This section aims to pique your curiosity and get your creative juices flowing. What would you be excited to build?

A unique intersection of opportunities you may have yet to consider may stand out here.

Instead of compiling an exhaustive reference list of all the different income streams you can create, I hand-picked particularly automatable businesses.

Although I tried to be as complete as possible, this is far from an exhaustive list, so keep your search to what's in this chapter. There are limitless new opportunities daily, so follow your curiosity and explore.

Types of Income

Let's start with an overview of the seven different types of income that you can create.

- **Earned income:** Income from your job
- **Rental income:** Income from renting out your commercial or residential property
- **Royalty income:** A passive income where you earn money based on the ongoing use or distribution of your intellectual property, can include: books, music, art, patents, photography, franchises, video content, or building and selling apps and software
- **Dividend income:** Income from owning dividend-paying stocks
- **Interest income:** Income from lending money
- **Capital gains income:** Income from selling assets that have increased in value
- **Profit income:** Income from buying and selling

We can primarily create these types of income through

our businesses and investments. Let's explore some business ideas.

Digital Business Ideas

- **Blogging:** Start a blog in a niche you're passionate about. Monetize it through affiliate marketing, sponsored posts, ads, and selling digital products like eBooks.
- **YouTube Channel:** Create and monetize engaging video content in a specific niche or on various topics, leveraging YouTube's vast audience to earn revenue through ads, sponsorships, and merchandise sales.
- **Kindle Publishing:** Write and self-publish books on Amazon's Kindle platform, catering to a wide range of genres and audiences, with the ability to earn passive income through direct sales and Kindle Unlimited readership.
- **Affiliate Marketing:** Promote products or services and earn a commission for each sale or lead you generate from blogging, YouTube videos, or social media.
- **Dropshipping:** Set up an online store where you sell products from suppliers who handle inventory and shipping. You focus on marketing and customer service.
- **High Ticket Online Courses:** Develop and sell in-depth, premium online courses in areas of your expertise, targeting professionals or enthusiasts willing to pay a higher price for advanced knowledge and skills.

- **Podcasting:** Start a podcast on a niche topic. Monetize through sponsorships, affiliate marketing, and selling branded merchandise.
- **Music Streaming:** Promote your music on music streaming platforms like Apple Music, Spotify, Deezer, and Amazon Music. These platforms pay royalties according to the number of streams your music receives.
- **Etsy Store:** Sell your handmade digital or physical products online through platforms like Etsy or your e-commerce website.

Real Estate Business Ideas

• **Short-Term Rentals:** Renting out your property for short-term stays, often through platforms like Airbnb, generates income through higher rental rates than traditional long-term leases.

• **Flipping:** Real estate flipping involves purchasing properties, often in need of repair or renovation, then improving them to sell at a higher price for a profit.

• **Property Management Services:** This business focuses on managing residential or commercial properties for owners, handling tasks like tenant placement, maintenance, and rent collection in exchange for a fee or percentage of the rent.

• **Real Estate Development:** Real estate development entails purchasing land or old properties to construct new buildings or significantly renovate existing structures, aiming to sell or lease the developed property for a profit.

Investment Ideas

• **Acorns:** A micro-investing platform that rounds up your everyday purchases to the nearest dollar and invests the difference, making it easy to start investing with small amounts.

• **Wealthfront:** Wealthfront is a robo-advisor investment platform offering automated, algorithm-driven financial planning and investment management services with minimal human intervention, catering to various financial goals from retirement to wealth building.

• **Fundrise:** Fundrise is an online real estate investment platform that allows individuals to invest in commercial and residential properties through a simple, accessible, and relatively low-cost model, leveraging the benefits of real estate investment trusts (REITs).

• **CrowdStreet:** A real estate investing platform that provides access to individual commercial real estate investment opportunities, allowing for direct investment in single properties.

• **Real Estate Investment Trusts (REITs):** Invest in REITs, companies that own, operate, and finance income-generating real estate. Earn dividends from the income-generating real estate projects held in the REIT without directly owning or managing them.

• **Stash:** A personal finance and investing app that helps beginners start investing with as little as $5, offering educational resources and various investment options.

• **Prosper:** A P2P lending platform that offers personal loans for various purposes, including debt consolidation, home improvements, and medical expenses, allowing investors to choose loans to fund based on risk tolerance and returns.

True Stories to Inspire

I would like to highlight a few inspirational stories of entrepreneurs who started businesses entirely based on seeing a problem that needed to be solved.

Hearing their stories teaches me that your business or income stream doesn't have to fit into a box. It can be a unique way for you to solve a problem in the world and express something beautiful to uplift and inspire others.

How Lisa Fink Makes $400,000 Per Year Selling Educational Printables

Lisa Fink taught for 15 years before leaving the classroom to work full-time on her educational printable business.

She identified a need for ready-to-use, engaging learning materials that save time and make learning more interactive and enjoyable. Her offerings, which include a range of printables like escape rooms, color by number, scavenger hunts, and digital secret message activities, have been widely embraced and downloaded over 250,000 times by a diverse customer base, including teachers, homeschool parents, and party planners.

What sets her business apart is her creativity and her passive income model. Once a printable is created and uploaded, it can generate revenue repeatedly with minimal additional effort. In fact, within just a few years of starting the business, she generated over $1 million in sales from her printables.

The Home Edit

The Home Edit transformed a common problem - household clutter - into a fun and thriving business with a memorable brand and multiple product lines.

The Home Edit was founded in 2015 by Clea Shearer and Joanna Teplin. The duo started the business to reinvent traditional organizing and merge it with design and interior styling.

Their color-coded and aesthetically driven approach was so successful that it created viral marketing.

Capitalizing on this success, they expanded their business model beyond services by launching a product line that includes organizing tools and resources, making their method accessible to a broader audience.

Furthermore, the partnership with Netflix to create a show allowed them to leverage media to showcase their tips and techniques live, further amplifying their reach and impact.

Although not officially disclosed, The Home Edit makes $1.47 million annually and has an estimated net worth of $7.37 million.

How Surbhi Sarna Built a $275 Million Biotech Company

Surbhi Sarna is an inspiring entrepreneur who founded nVision Medical, a company that developed a groundbreaking microcatheter to detect ovarian cancer. At age 13, she suffered from ovarian cysts so painful that they made her faint, and at the time, there wasn't a way for doctors to be able to tell if the cysts were cancerous. Undaunted, she vowed to create a new technology that would be able to detect ovarian cancer quickly and early. Her journey with nVision involved raising $17 million in venture funding, completing three clinical trials, and obtaining two first-in-class FDA approvals. The success of nVision culminated in its acquisition by Boston Scientific for $275 million, more than 15 times the invested money.

These are just a few inspirations. The abundance of entrepreneurial innovation is truly inspiring. I hope this section helped get the creative juices flowing. After taking some time to reflect and explore, let's assume the next step.

Step 2. Write down all the income streams that resonate with you

1. As you're exploring all the various income streams, reflect on which ones resonate with you.
2. Consider your inclination — are you more inclined towards business ownership? Investment? Both?
3. Visualize your life with your seven streams of income. What does it look like? Visualize and make sure it feels right.

What does your life look like for each of these income streams? How big do you want to grow them? What does the ultimate success look like for each one of them?

Step 3. Make a plan for how you're going to take each income stream from 0 to 1

VISUALIZE Your Success

What does success look like for each income stream if

you knew you couldn't fail? Work backward from your vision of success and break it down into three milestones. What are the three major milestones you need to reach for that outcome?

Plan

What first step can you take to progress towards your first significant milestone? What can you do for 30 days to make this come to life? What can you do today?

Act

Create a table or spreadsheet with the following structure to support you in brainstorming your income streams, your ultimate vision for each one, and how you will work backward to make it happen.

Income Stream	Ultimate Vision	Milestones	Next Step
This can be anything that generates money for you, it can be your day job, business ventures, investments, and savings accounts.	What is an ultimate vision for this income stream that absolutely excites you?	What are 3 key milestones to get from where you are now to your ultimate vision?	What is an impactful next step that you can take today?

Income Stream: Anything that generates money for you, such as your day job, business ventures, investments, and savings accounts.

Ultimate Vision: What is an ultimate vision for this income stream that excites you?

Milestones: What are three critical milestones from where you are now to your ultimate vision?

Next Step: What is an impactful next step you can take today?

The Most Exciting 3 Cents I Ever Made

When I started building my income streams, I wanted to get into real estate. But at the time, I didn't have enough savings to create a real estate business, and I had given myself a 30-day deadline, so I had to come up with something fast.

With only 30 days to take action on this goal, I searched for ways to invest in real estate with a small amount of capital and discovered Fundrise, an online investment platform that allows you to invest in real estate with as little as $10. This was exactly what I needed at the time.

Following my challenge, I created an account, set aside $100, and celebrated creating a new income stream.

A few days later, I remember excitedly texting my sisters, "Look! I made 0.03c in dividend payments without doing anything! My money is already working for me!"

I don't know if anyone else could ever be as excited about making their first 0.03c passive income, but I was psyched! It was a step in the right direction, and I love celebrating a good win. "My money is already working hard for me," I joked with pride.

This tiny 0.03c dividend payment illustrated a mental shift from "I work hard for my money" to "my money is working hard for me."

Over the past five years, I've steadily built up six income streams, and the launch of this book is officially my seventh income stream. I've expanded my original seven streams to make the groundwork for about a dozen income streams in the form of various businesses and investments I'd like to create one day. But it all started with committing to massive action in 30 days, and those 0.03c were the seeds that grew into something much greater.

Conclusion

Creating seven streams of income in 30 days is ambitious and exciting. But the first 30 days are just a launching pad to take massive action towards the bigger picture vision of who you want to be.

It's okay to start small, even if it means investing $10, $100, or $1000. Celebrate the milestones of creating new streams of income. Celebrate your money working for you. What else can you create?

I hope you have doubled or tripled your income streams by the end of this challenge. I hope you have explored new avenues of income, new business ideas to generate, and new investments to partake in. You will have exercised and built muscle for brainstorming and creating income streams.

Initially, seven income streams may seem like a lot, but over time, your mind will start to get used to generating new ideas and be inclined to focus on building. It will come naturally. Next thing you know, you'll have multiple income streams that you're working on in parallel.

In this book's final section, we will go over three hand-picked streams of income, specifically businesses, that anyone can start with minimum capital investment and scale and automate with GPT and Retool.

6

INCOME STREAM: HIGH-TICKET ONLINE COURSES

"Whether you think you're worth a hundred dollars or a thousand dollars, you're right." — *Danielle Leslie*

What is a high-ticket online course? A high-ticket online course is a premium course targeting professionals or enthusiasts willing to pay a higher price for advanced knowledge and skills. High-ticket courses typically sell for $2000 or more.

Valuable as they are, we want to differentiate against the $129 courses you can buy on Udemy. Popular courses on Udemy like *The Complete 2023 Web Development Bootcamp ($123), Practical Leadership Skills ($129)*, and *Microsoft Excel from Beginner to Advanced ($129)* are valuable. Still, the scope of these courses is specific to technical and business skills acquisition.

In contrast, high-ticket online courses sell a significant transformation by teaching you a new skillset that unlocks multiples over the $2000 course investment. Let's take a look at some examples.

High Ticket Course Inspirations

Sam Ovens, consulting.com

Sam Ovens specializes in teaching you how to start your own consulting business and grow it into a multi-million dollar business. He teaches how to differentiate from being a generic freelancer to a highly specialized consultant, for which you can charge a premium. He also teaches you how to max out your book of business and decouple yourself from charging hourly, both essential lessons for making the transition from getting started with freelancing to being a highly sought-after specialized consultant. I took his course in 2018 and grew my business from $100k/year to $210k/year. I paid $2k for the course, which was well worth the outcome of a $100k increase in annual earnings. One of the things that stood out to me was his marketing and how his course had successfully created 52 millionaire students. Sam himself has also made over $34 million a year.

Danielle Leslie, coursefromscratch.com

I learned about Danielle Leslie through Sam's program and was so inspired by her that I had to take her course and try it out for myself. Initially, Danielle worked on course marketing for Udemy, where she learned what makes a course marketable and what makes a course sell. In Course From Scratch, she teaches you the framework she uses to create and launch a course for $20,000 in 60 days. She teaches you how to identify your unique course topic and launch a profitable *minimum viable course*, methodically validating that your market will buy your course before you begin creating course content. Danielle is an energizing and insightful teacher to learn from, and her method works! Following her method, I ran a pilot and made $5000 on my first-course launch. Danielle has done over $20 million in course sales.

Brian Page, bnbformula.com

Brian Page's course teaches you how to make $300,000 a year by creating an Airbnb short-term rental empire without owning any property. He teaches you how to identify attractive short-term rentals, lease them, list them on Airbnb, and then automate the entire business. His online course also goes into the specifics of automating an Airbnb rental business. Launching this online course was successful for Brian, as he made over $1 million in course sales within the first six weeks.

UNLIKE COURSES that teach technical or business skills, with these high-ticket online courses, what you're selling is transformation. Although all the examples above are business courses, I don't want you to think that all high-ticket online courses have to be about starting lucrative businesses. Successful students from Danielle Leslie's program sell high-ticket courses for various topics, including acting workshops, photography, writing and publishing, personal finance, health and fitness, parenting, and spirituality.

Why start a high-ticket online course business in 2023?

1. Online learning is a fast-growing market with a lot of demand

The global massive open online course (MOOC) market experienced substantial growth, increasing from $12.54 billion in 2022 to $16.73 billion in 2023. The United States holds a significant portion of the online learning market, accounting for about 34% of the online learning platform market globally. The US eLearning market is expected to grow by $21.64 billion by 2024.

Online learning has grown tremendously since its inception and will likely continue to grow as people intuitively search for courses, knowledge, and information online.

The way we learn has changed. Instead of going to a school to learn new skills, it's intuitive for us to open YouTube and do initial searches for what's already out there before investing in more formalized learning. Specifically, we're looking to learn from experts who have done what we are looking to do.

A hungry, fast-growing market means that people are searching for and wanting to buy new content that shows them how to reach their goals.

2. Everybody has a course within them

I truly believe that everybody has at least one (if not multiple) unique courses within them that only they can teach. Your unique and special combination of passions, professional skills, hobbies, and biggest life learnings can truly help those getting started on the path where you were once a beginner. You can truly be creative and design a course around anything, whether it's a hobby you're passionate about or a change that you wish to enable in the world.

3. Sell Less, Make More

How many courses would you need to sell to make $1 million if they were all $2000 courses?

In contrast, how many courses would you need to sell to make $1 million if they were all $49 courses?

You would need 500 customers at the $2000 price point and 20,408 customers at the $49 price point.

By the numbers alone, a high-ticket online course could be a fast path towards becoming a GPT millionaire.

4. Low cost to get started

Starting a high-ticket online course is very accessible and low-cost to get started. Not only that but if you follow a minimum viable course launch method, you're *already getting paid* upfront by your customers to validate your own business model.

6. Automatable with AI

Last but not least, this business is very automatable with AI. Marketing will really drive success in this business, and AI can help us create our marketing materials faster.

6 Ways to Automate High Ticket Online Courses with AI

In this section, we're going to share six gems; each one is an idea for how you could automate aspects of your high-ticket online course business.

Gem 1: Use your student's challenges to create compelling course & marketing content

A common blind spot for entrepreneurs and course creators is that we may actually forget the challenges that we faced as beginners. As experts today, we may not even think of some of our students' challenges as actual challenges. We can use ChatGPT to identify and create a variety of materials to help our students address these challenges.

Here is a series of prompts you can use to get ahead of students' challenges, understand the keywords they would be searching to find a solution, and then create course modules and blog posts addressing those challenges.

HERE IS a flow you can use:

Prompt 1: I'm going to be creating a course to help {persona} achieve {outcome}. What are some of the biggest challenges that {persona} may have?

Prompt 2: What are some search queries or keywords that a {persona} who is struggling with {topic} might type into Google?

Prompt 3: Can you create an outline of a course module for me on {challenge}?

Prompt 4: Can you create a blog post for me featuring tips on addressing {challenge}?

Gem 2: Automating blog and social media content creation

Continuing with the example, let's say you now have a list of student's key challenges in the form of topics or keywords.

Using the structure we learned in Chapter 4, you could build a Retool app and workflow that ingests these keywords and generates a series of blog posts and social media posts for you to review.

Upon review, you could designate a blog post or social media post ready for production and use your blogging API or social media API to post to production on a schedule.

As an extra credit, you could vectorize your existing blog and social media content so that your prompts can reference your writing style and previous information you have shared with your students and followers.

Gem 3: Automate all aspects of your course content creation

What if you created a suite of apps that automated your course creation process? You could create an app for course materials, workshop outlines, and homework generation.

In the Retool app builder, you can use a Navigation Bar component to bring all your apps together into a suite of tools.

Here are some prompts to get you going.

Course Module Prompts
Prompt: I'm teaching an online course on {course topic}. My students are having challenges with {challenge}. Can you create a

course module on how to {address challenge} to {achieve outcome}?

Example Prompt: I'm teaching an online course on how to make six figures for the first time. My students are having challenges with facing fear when negotiating their salary. Can you create a course module on how to face their fears to negotiate a higher salary?

Workshop Outline Prompts
Prompt: Can you help me design a workshop on {topic}?

Homework Prompts
Prompt: Can you create an outline of homework to give to my students to help them {face challenge}?

Gem 4: Automate your email marketing to convert prospects into students

One of your marketing motions may likely be maintaining an email marketing list of prospects who may have engaged with your content on your YouTube channel or website but who may not yet have officially purchased your course.

You can generate an entire nurture and conversion campaign by taking each challenge that your student may be facing and writing a short email about how your course teaches them to overcome that challenge.

At the end of the email or story, you could invite them to take action by signing up for the course in order to fully face and address the challenge.

Here is a flow you can use to generate three weeks of email marketing.

Nurture Email Prompt Flow (Abstracted)
Prompt 1: You are an expert email marketer. Outline an email marketing campaign for a course on {how to achieve outcome}. In this email marketing campaign, I want to write one email a week to nurture my prospects into buying my online course by writing a short email about the challenges they may be facing and how my course can help them overcome those challenges.

Here is the list of challenges they are facing as students who want to {achieve the outcome that my course promises}:
1. {challenge 1}
2. {challenge 2}
3. {challenge 3}

Prompt 2: Great! Now, you are an expert copywriter. Draft the first email for me using friendly and encouraging language.

Here is the same flow above, but using the concrete example of a course that teaches people how to make six figures for the first time.

Nurture Email Prompt Flow (Concrete Example)
Prompt 1: Outline an email marketing campaign for I'm teaching a course on how to make six figures for the first time. In this email marketing campaign, I want to write one email a week to nurture my prospects into buying my online course by writing a short email about the challenges they may be facing and how my course can help them overcome those challenges.

Here is the list of challenges they are facing as students who want to make six figures for the first time:
1. skill and experience gap: investing time and energy to acquire new skills in a new field or in a more challenging field

2. work-life balance: fear of longer hours and more demanding work

3. imposter syndrome: feeling self-doubt and fear of failure

Prompt 2: Great! Now, you are an expert copywriter. Draft the first email for me using friendly and encouraging language.

With this approach, you are adding value to your prospects with every email you send.

Gem 5: Build a custom tutor for your students

As a teacher, you may likely get asked the same questions by your students again and again. If you also manage a community or Facebook Group, you may find that your students post the same questions again and again without referencing previous posts.

What if your students were able to search and actually find the answers for themselves? You could build a custom tutor for your students using Retool Vectors and the Chat Component. Not only would your students learn how to fish, but this could save you and your team a lot of time from answering the same questions. Now, let's walk through how you could build a minimum viable prototype of this on Retool in just minutes.

1. First, using Retool Vectors, vectorize your Q&A, transcriptions of your office hours, and Facebook group posts.

2. Second, create a chat interface by simply dragging and dropping the Chat Component onto the canvas.

3. Third, make sure that the AI query that is connected to the chat component is referencing your vectors. And that's it! Give it a try, and you should be able to get answers to your questions.

Here is a screenshot of what your prototype could look like. In the example below, we vectorized our Facebook Group, Office Hour Transcriptions, and Student FAQ. We dragged a Chat Component onto the canvas and referenced the relevant vectors. Athat'st's it! The rest of the chat component functionality comes out of the box.

Taking this into production may mean more time invested in vectorizing your content. You can programmatically vectorize your content (ex: every office hour automatically gets transcribed into text and then vectorized via a workflow and then added to your "Office Hour Transcriptions" folder).

Gem 6: YouTube video script creation

YouTube is the most-used social media platform among Generation Z, with a significant 88% of them spending time on the app.

YouTube is no longer just a platform for entertainment

but a medium for learning and discovery. Among Gen Z, YouTube has changed the way we find and learn new things. Instead of searching Google first, we may be more likely to search on YouTube first. Having our videos there can be a valuable marketing channel for us to meet our potential students while they're actively looking for the course we have to offer.

Let's say you want to do a YouTube video series for your online course. This could require a meaningful time investment if done entirely from scratch.

We can use ChatGPT to save us time by automating the following:

1) high performing keyword discovery related to our online course

2) YouTube script content creation

3) YouTube video metadata content creation

Keyword Discovery Prompts

Prompt 1 (Abstract): I'm creating a video series for my YouTube channel to target potential students for my online course on how to {course outcome}. What are some high search volume keywords for YouTube that my potential students may be typing to search for content on how to {course outcome}?

Prompt 1 (Concrete): I'm creating a video series for my YouTube channel to target potential students for my online course on {how to make six figures for the first time}. What are some high search volume keywords for YouTube that my potential students may be typing to search for content on how to make six figures? Be sure to include the estimated monthly search volume in your answer.

Prompt 2 (Abstract): What are ten popular questions related to {course outcome}?

Prompt 2 (Concrete): What are ten popular questions related to making six figures for the first time?

Prompt 3 (Abstract): What are ten common misconceptions about {course topic}?
Prompt 3 (Concrete): What are ten common misconceptions about making six figures for the first time?

YouTube Video Script Creation Prompts
Prompt 1: Write a script for a YouTube tutorial video on {topic}.

Prompt 2 (Abstract): Write a script for a YouTube video about common misconceptions related to {course outcome}. In this video, I'm going to be overturning the following misconception: {misconception}. In the script, highlight three reasons why this misconception isn't true and invite the student to take my course at the end of the video.

Prompt 2 (Concrete): Write a script for a YouTube video about common misconceptions related to {making six figures for the first time}. In this video, I'm going to be overturning the following misconception: {that you must be born into wealth to make six figures}. In the script, highlight three reasons why this misconception isn't true and invite the student to take my course at the end of the video.

YouTube Video Metadata
YouTube video metadata consists of your Video Title, Description, Time Stamps, Tags, Category, and Thumbnail. Writing metadata can be time-intensive, so this is a great task to automate.

Out the gates, ChatGPT can write comprehensive metadata with very little guidance on your part.

Prompt 1: Create the metadata for my YouTube video on {topic}.

To create even more automation and save even more time, you could create a workflow that automatically writes your metadata based on the title, tags, and category that you likely have pre-defined in your keyword research phase.

Conclusion

High-ticket online courses are a great potential income stream to consider adding to your portfolio. The online learning market is growing fast, and many people are likely already searching for what you have to offer on YouTube and other channels. Everyone has a course within them and a unique insight they can share with the world. Your high-ticket online course can truly elevate people's lives by showing them that not only are their dreams possible but that you have a direct path to getting there. This business model is very accessible to start. You can even get paid upfront to validate your course idea if you choose to follow a minimum viable course launch model. Last but not least, you can automate various aspects of this business with AI, from course module creation to email marketing campaigns to building an AI tutor for your students to be able to answer their own questions. As Danielle Leslie said, *"Whether you think you're worth a hundred dollars or a thousand dollars, you're right."* Why not give the thousand-dollar course model a try?

7

INCOME STREAM: BLOGGING

"Being able to touch so many people through my business and make money while doing it, is a huge blessing." — *Magic Johnson*

I know you're probably wondering, "Blogging in 2023? Do people still make money blogging in 2023?" I had similar skepticism until working on this book because my impression of blogs was a bit dated. Until I found out how much bloggers make in 2023.

According to ZipRecruiter, the average blogger makes about $45,000 a year, with most bloggers earning between $38,050 and $51,000. It's not bad for an additional income stream that is relatively automatable. On the high end, some of the most famous bloggers in the world make millions of dollars a year, so this is a niche that you can invest your time in automating.

Why start a blog in 2023?

1. Low cost & easy to get started

Blogging is an accessible income stream because of the low initial upfront cost and the ability to automate a significant part of the business with AI.

Anyone can get started blogging while still working on their day job. There are endless niches and topics that you can blog about. You can help people learn a new hobby, develop their careers, learn a new skill or craft, create more joy in their relationships, or deepen their spiritual practice.

2. Monetize your blog with multiple revenue streams

You can monetize your blog with various revenue streams. Here are some ideas to get your creative juices flowing:

• **Advertising:** You could use ad networks to place ads directly on your blog. You could also sell ad space directly to companies looking to reach your audience.

• **Affiliate Marketing:** You could promote related products and services in various forms and earn a commission for every sale or lead you generate.

• **Sponsored Content:** You could collaborate with brands to create one-time sponsored content that promotes their brand, product, or services to your audience.

• **Selling Digital Products:** You can sell eBooks, courses, webinars, and digital downloads.

• **Selling Physical Products:** You can use the blog as a launch point to sell a physical product line to your audience.

• **Services:** Sell services related to your expertise

(resume review, website design, marketing consulting).

• **Subscription Model:** Create and sell a subscription offering, whether premium content or a physical product.

3. Build and nurture an audience that you can sell to

Blogging allows you to build and nurture an audience to cross-sell your other products and services. For example, if you're looking to launch a high-ticket online course on a particular topic, you could concurrently start a blog that markets to potential students interested in your course.

4. You can fast-track consistent monetization by creating recurring sponsorships with corporations

Corporate marketers are always looking for new channels to reach a wider audience. It is even better if they can keep those channels on the docket for a few months and generate consistent returns from an investment in that channel. If you have established your niche, you can start reaching out to corporations directly that you can work with on long-term marketing campaigns that can simultaneously add value to your audience and be financially successful for you and your corporate sponsor. Early-stage venture-backed start-ups that have just recently closed a round of funding are likely eager to look for creative ways to invest that funding in marketing campaigns.

5. Blogging can be a jump-off point to a much larger business

Blogging can be your jump-off point to creating a much larger business. By focusing on adding value to your readers and cultivating an audience, you open the door to incredible opportunities in the future.

From Law Student Blogger to Fashion Empire $20M Net Worth

Chiara Ferragni was a law student when she started her blog, The Blonde Salad, in 2009. It was a mix of fashion, beauty, and lifestyle. Ferragni's unique style and keen sense of branding and audience engagement quickly garnered a massive following. Her blog's success opened doors to numerous high-profile collaborations with leading fashion brands, elevating her status in the fashion world. Leveraging her growing influence, Ferragni expanded her reach by launching her namesake fashion lines, which are internationally recognized and have an estimated net worth of $20 million across all her businesses.

From Mark's Daily Apple to $200M Acquisition

Mark Sisson founded his blog, Mark's Daily Apple, in 2006. It focused on getting healthy and fit by eating clean food, lifting heavy weights, and spending time outdoors. Initially, Mark monetized his blog by offering digital products but quickly realized that people needed better nutrition. He started selling supplements but realized he could do more. Mark realized that what set his dishes apart were the sauces and marinades he used to finish them. He realized that most sauces and marinades on grocery shelves were made with artificial ingredients, which led to the creation of Primal Kitchen, his line of sauces and dressings with all-natural ingredients. Primal Kitchen was a huge success. You may have seen or even purchased Primal Kitchen products at your local grocery store. I sure have! Mark sold Primal Kitchen to Kraft Foods for $200 million in 2019. Since Mark had been growing his audience from his blog since 2006, he retained majority control over the business during this acquisition.

Blogging can serve as a starting point for building a larger business. By providing valuable content to your readers and building an audience, you create the path for exciting future opportunities.

6. Blogging is extremely automatable with AI

Last but not least, blogging is *highly* automatable with AI. From keyword research to blog post creation to social media post creation, you can automate a significant amount of content creation, freeing up your time and mental energy to focus on working on the business.

7 Ways to Automate Blogging with AI

Getting started with blogging in 2023 is a different ball game than ever.

Gem 1: Blog post topic generation

Prompt 1: I'm looking to start a blog at the intersection of {topic 1} and {topic 2}. What are ten great ideas for blog posts that I should consider?

Prompt 2: On the topic of {blog topic}, what are key challenges that people may face when getting started? Draft a blog post title for each challenge.

Prompt 3: I'm going to start a {topic} blog. What are key trends in 2024 that I might want to blog about? List them out as blog post titles.

Prompt 4: I'm starting a blog on {topic}. What are common questions people may have as they begin with {topic}? List them out as blog post titles.

Prompt 5: I'm starting a blog on {topic}. What are some how-to guides that I should consider writing for my blog?

Gem 2: Automate writing your blog posts

Remember when we created a simple blog post generator app that took a list of topics and fired off a custom workflow to write a blog post for each topic?

Here are a few ideas for building on that original application to further automate the content generation side of the business.

1. Create and optimize different workflows for structuring various types of blog posts. For example, Listicles, How-Tos, Checklists, and Ultimate Guides are structures we can model and customize uniquely to fit our brand and audience.

2. Add a block to our workflow that appends SEO-optimized keywords and metadata.

3. Add a block to our workflow that shapes the blog with all its SEO keywords and metadata in the proper HTML format to post directly to our blogging platform.

Gem 3: Keyword research & SEO optimization

Instead of learning and navigating keyword research plat-forms, use ChatGPT to quickly get lists of keywords you can start with to get your blog off the ground.

Below are some prompts to get started, with particular credit to Corey Frankosky from Surfside PPC for Prompt 2; it's fantastic.

Prompt 1: What are the top keywords related to {topic} that will drive traffic to our blog and increase search engine visibility?

Prompt 2: I am creating content on my blog about {target keyword}. I want to teach my readers everything about {target keyword} and rank high on Google for popular long-tail keywords related to the short-tail keyword {target keyword}. Suggest 30 long-tail keyword ideas for {target keyword} that will be helpful topics for people who read my blog posts.

Prompt 3: What are the ten most popular sub-topics related to {topic}?

Prompt 4: Here is a list of keywords that have done well in my most successful posts. Generate suggestions for related keywords with a high search volume but low competition so I can create more content that will likely perform well.

Gem 4: Image creation

You can use DALL-E and Midjourney to automate the creation of thematically consistent images for your blogs.

Although Midjourney does not have an official API, you can access DALL-E's API directly in Retool.

To create images as part of your workflows, you'll want to add a new Retool AI block to your workflow and select "Generate image" under the Action type.

To create images as part of an app, write a new query, select AI Action, and specify Generate Image as your Action type.

Gem 5: Automatically generate social media posts to promote your blog post

We covered email marketing and YouTube video script automation in the previous chapter. To round out our marketing automation examples, you can build on your blog post workflow by automatically generating social media posts in parallel across all platforms at the end of your workflow.

Here is an example of a workflow block generating an Instagram post for you.

At the end of your workflow, you can generate all your social media posts in parallel, as shown below.

Gem 6: Use ChatGPT to create more leverage by understanding and repeating what's working

If something works, it just makes sense to do more of it and repeat what's already working. To do this before ChatGPT, we would likely be going through our analytics data, stalking competitor blogs, and doing extensive Google Keyword Research to see if there were any keywords and topics we might have missed. We can save tremendous time by cutting straight to the chase of what's working and then using GPT to brainstorm ways to remix and continue what's already working.

Here are some prompt ideas for identifying and repeating your success.

Prompt 1: Here is my blog's performance data, including page views, bounce rates, time on site, and social media engagement. Based on the data, what patterns or trends do you observe about which types of posts are most popular and engaging? Generate suggestions for similar posts that may perform well.

Prompt 2: Here is a list of keywords I've used in my most successful posts. Generate suggestions for related keywords or topics with a high search volume but low competition, helping you create content that is likely to perform well.

Prompt 3: Here are the top-performing headlines across all my blog posts. What makes these headlines so successful? Suggest new ones for future posts based on these successful patterns.

Prompt 4: Here are the top competitors in my niche. Can you analyze them and tell me what they are doing well? Give me ideas for improving my content to do just as well, if not better, than my competitors.

Prompt 5: These are my highest-performing blog posts. Suggest ways to repurpose this content into other formats like videos, infographics, podcasts, etc.

Gem 7: Explore and identify creative and impactful blog monetization strategies with the help of AI

By automating a lot of our content creation, we free up time to be more strategic in working on our business. One of the critical areas we can work on is improving our blog's monetization and business. ChatGPT can be a great brainstorming partner and starting point for some of these higher-leverage initiatives.

Here are some ideas for starting a conversation and opening ideas for improving monetization:

Prompt 1: I'm creating a blog on {topic}. I currently work with {company} as an affiliate. What are other affiliates that I might want to consider working with? What creative ways can I create blog posts that convert for these affiliates?

Prompt 2: I'm creating a blog on {topic} targeting {audience}. What are some digital product ideas that I could make for my audience?

Prompt 3: I'm looking to grow the monetization of my blog on {topic}. What are upcoming seasonal trends that I can prepare creative content around that might monetize well, given the season? Generate three blog post ideas for me based on each

seasonal trend and specify how this post could improve mone-
tization.

Prompt 4: I've grown my blog to an audience of {key demo-
graphic} interested in {topics of interest}. What are some brands,
start-ups, or companies that might want to work with me in a
strategic capacity to create custom campaigns? For each corpora-
tion, generate three ideas for campaigns that we could run
together that would be massively successful.

Prompt 5: I'm considering running a campaign called {campaign
name} for my blog. In this campaign, I would partner with
{brand} and {influencer} to create a new label of designer clothes
that we sell under the {campaign name} label. How can this idea
come to life and generate millions of dollars in revenue?

But wait, there's more: real-life millionaire bloggers

Building on the stories of Chiara Ferragni and Mark Sisson,
I wanted to share a few more inspiring millionaire bloggers
to show the art of the possible.

Smart Passive Income by Pat Flynn ($2mm/year)

Pat Flynn's journey is a classic tale of turning adversity into
opportunity. After getting laid off as an architect in 2008,
Flynn started Smart Passive Income, determined to take
control of his destiny. "I worked so hard in that industry, and
I still got kicked out. I thought it was secure, but it was not. I
have to take control." His transparent approach to sharing
his income sources and strategies resonated with readers.
What started as a humble blog documenting his income-
generating experiments has grown into a multi-million

dollar empire, educating and inspiring countless individuals to explore passive income opportunities.

Neil Patel ($1mm/year & $30mm net worth)

Neil Patel's story is one of relentless innovation and marketing savvy. He began his journey as a passionate marketer and, out of the gates, co-founded multiple businesses, including Crazy Egg, KISSmetrics, and Neil Patel Digital. His blog, known for detailed and actionable marketing advice, has become a go-to resource for companies and entrepreneurs. His advice is just honest, and it's good. With an estimated value of around $30 million, Patel exemplifies how skill, determination, and a knack for digital marketing can lead to substantial success.

Conclusion

It's a new era for blogging. With average bloggers making $43k/year to creating multi-million dollar empires and $200m+ exits, blogging is not an income stream to be missed, especially in 2023, with AI at our fingertips. Keyword research, blog post creation, social media creation, and monetization are more automatable than ever. Add to that the fun of starting and building a blog you're passionate about that could inspire and uplift millions. Blogs are incredibly monetizable and make great launch pads for entrepreneurial ventures in almost any industry. Anything is possible. What blog would you start if you knew you couldn't fail? "The best time to plant a tree was 20 years ago. The second best time is now."

8

INCOME STREAM: KINDLE DIRECT PUBLISHING

"The secret of getting ahead is getting started." — *Mark Twain*

Kindle Direct Publishing (KDP) is Amazon's self-publishing platform. It's a way to independently self-publish your book on the Amazon platform and get in front of Amazon's 310 million customers worldwide.

KDP self-publishing businesses make my top 3 accessible income streams anyone can build. Like high-ticket online courses and blogging, it's very accessible to get started, highly automatable, and an exitable venture with acquisitions ranging from $1 million to $3 million.

Self-publishing excites me because it's like owning real estate online. In America, 63% of consumers start their search for a new product on Amazon. If you can identify niches with high search volume and a reasonable amount of competition that you're willing to go up against, it's fair game! Once your book is published and your marketing systems are automated, you collect monthly royalties, a genuinely passive income stream. You can build and grow your business by selling more books in a series, expanding to new niches, and expanding to different types of books (paperback, audiobook, and multiple language translations).

eBook publishing is currently a $16.42 billion market that is expected to grow to $32 billion in 2032. What's driving all this growth?

On the consumer side, more and more people prefer to buy eBooks because you can instantly access the content and read it from your tablet or device. It's much faster and easier than going to a store to buy a physical book, ordering it online, and then waiting for it to get delivered.

As a publisher, you can get instant global distribution and reach with ebooks and self-publishing, reaching a wider audience faster without worrying about physical book distribution.

Overall, this is good news for us! Despite what may seem like a saturated market, there's a lot of room for people to create fresh new content and build empires.

Real-Life KDP Millionaires

What inspires me about these success stories is the balance between those who achieved success because they were focused on building a publishing *business* and those who achieved success because they were passionate about mastering the craft of writing.

Sean Dollwet, Royalty Hero

Sean Dollwet built his publishing business from zero to millionaire in five years by focusing on consistently publishing high-quality books on KDP. He grew his company to $40k/mo in revenue and sold it for $820,000. Today, he runs Royalty Hero, an online course that teaches students how to start, scale, and exit their own KDP self-publishing businesses.

Additionally, Sean recently started a *new* KDP business while growing Royalty Hero and is transparently sharing metrics to show his students that he is the real deal! Six months in, he has already developed his new KDP business to generate $20k/mo while outsourcing as much as possible to automate the time he spends on the business to 30 minutes a day.

Rachel Richards, Money Honey

Rachel Richards started her career as a financial advisor. She noticed that people in her life constantly came to her for help with their finances. Rachel realized that many financial books could have been more exciting and written with young women's needs in mind. She began writing Money Honey in 2017 and self-published the book in September. Immediately, the book started consistently bringing in $1000 per month.

Alongside founding a successful real estate company and making enough money to be able to retire in 3 years from her rental income, she self-published her second book, *Passive Income, Aggressive Retirement,* and to date has sold over $100k in royalties annually from her self-publishing income stream. Today, she lives off her $20,000 per month of passive income.

Joseph Alexander, Self-Published Millionaire

Joseph Alexander is a musician and author of over 40 books on playing the guitar. As part of his self-publishing business, he has published over 120 books in six years, earning over $2,500,000 in royalties. His tuition books are published in four languages and have sold over 1,000,000 copies to widespread critical acclaim.

He is a publisher of over 200 music books, and his label, Fundamental Changes, is currently accepting manuscripts from a new talented generation of musicians and offers 3x the standard royalty rates to educators.

Today, he published a book called Self-Published Millionaire, telling his story of going from a private guitar teacher to consistently generating over $2,000 a day in royalties.

Amanda Hocking, Millionaire Paranormal Fiction Writer

It all started when Amanda needed to raise a few hundred dollars when, in desperation, she made her unpublished novel available for sale on Kindle. At first, she started selling one or two books a day, and then six months later, it all exploded. She sold 6,000 books in one month and then sold $9,000 per month consistently.

Before she knew it, she crossed her one million book sale on Amazon Kindle and made over $2 million doing it. She also signed a multi-million dollar deal with St. Martin's Press to publish her first book, Switched.

Amanda's advice? "It's not enough to have a passion — you must have a work ethic. That's been the most life-changing advice that I got, because I had a passion for writing — and I know a lot of other people do, too — but it's not enough to just want something. You have to be able to work for it, too, and put in the hours and the time."

Whether you're a business owner looking to start and run a self-publishing business as a business or whether you're passionate about guitar or paranormal fiction, there are infinite possibilities for your success.

Why start a KDP self-publishing company in 2023?

1. You don't have to be a writer, and you don't need a degree to self-publish on Amazon

It may be surprising that you don't have to be a writer to self-publish on Amazon. You can publish many different types of books, not just novels. A popular niche of books to self-publish is called low-content books.

Low-content books are a category of books that have minimal written content. Journals, log books, planners, organizers, and coloring books are different types of low-content books you don't need a writer to publish.

You need to know how to do keyword research and identify niches where there is meaningful demand and competition. Besides that, you could also easily automate the generation of low-content books with AI.

Sue Irven and her husband make $17,000 monthly selling low-content books like journals, notebooks, and coloring books on KDP.

"My husband and I started selling on Amazon KDP in June 2020 and saw a profit after our very first month. KDP now serves as our full-time income," says Irvin.

The duo publishes about ten new designs a week using Canva. Their best sellers include composition notebooks, sketchbooks, journals, planners, and to-do lists. Today, they have published over 200 book designs that generate the bulk of their $17k per month. Self-publishing is a business anyone can get into, no matter their background.

2. *Low barrier to entry and flexes with your time*

Self-publishing has a low barrier to entry and is a low cost to getting started. Investing in writers, book cover designers, and managing ad budgets is optional. You can do all of these things yourself, but outsourcing as much as possible and focusing on optimizing the business can get you to your revenue goals much faster.

Self-publishing is also flexible with your time. You can put in as little or as much time as you want. You can make progress working on the business 2 hours a week or full-time. You can quickly start doing it on the side and scale up the hours you invest in your business.

3. *The business is entirely automatable, passive income, and excitable*

Self-publishing is completely automatable. You can hire a marketer to do keyword research and niche identification, a writer to ghostwrite your books, a designer to design your book covers, and another marketer to run your launch campaign and ongoing ad optimization.

You can build a genuinely passive income via royalties as you create more books in a successful series and expand to new niches, book types, formats (paperback, audiobook), and new markets.

A business that is fully automated is excitable. Sean Dollwet discusses going rates for these businesses in the

$1mm-$3mm range. Overall, this business checks all the boxes.

4. Leverage your strengths, passions, and hobbies

Whether you're a guitar expert or passionate about paranormal romance, whether you're a writer or not, you can follow your passion and find your audience via self-publishing. Self-publishing can be a unique and financially rewarding way to build a life-changing business and express your gift to the world.

3 Ways to Automate Self-Publishing with AI

Gem 1: Explore & identify profitable niches and trends in the eBook market

How does one find good niches for self-publishing? Typically, you would pull up a keyword research tool, go straight into Amazon, and start looking at metrics, data, and competitors. But this assumes that you already know what niche to begin searching.

What if you're looking to explore uncharted territory based on past bestsellers?

You can use ChatGPT to proactively explore interesting niches and creative book ideas before getting into the weeds of keyword search.

Fiction Topic Exploration

Prompt 1: I'm thinking of writing a young adult fiction ebook series, and I'm curious about current trending niches. Can you tell me about today's top 5 hottest or trending niches in young adult fiction?

Prompt 2: What are fast-growing sub-genres of {niche} that I can consider?

Prompt 3: What are some creative and unexpected ideas for a novel that blends both {genre 1} and {genre 2} that features {trend that is trending today}?

Non-Fiction Topic Exploration

Prompt: I noticed that {trend} is a very popular topic and growing trend. For example, {Best Selling Book} is incredibly successful, as is {Top Performing Show} on Netflix. I want to write a best-selling book on {trend} as well. What creative approaches can I consider taking? What are some unexpected or unusual ideas for positioning my book?

Gem 2: Automate manuscript outlining

MANUSCRIPT OUTLINING CAN BE one of the most painful and time-intensive parts of creating a high-content book. For some reason, it feels like you have to "create an entire manuscript out of nothing," and writer's block can hit hard!

In the same way that we built a blog post generator app by feeding it topics and having a workflow generate our blog post for us in the background, we could also create an automatic manuscript outline generator by providing keywords and having a workflow generate our manuscript outline.

From there, we can review the manuscript, ensuring it's what we want it to be and exploring creative angles and perspectives to create a truly and uniquely valuable book for our readers.

Gem 3: Optimize your book title & listings

Use ChatGPT to help you create an impactful book title. Save time by having it drafted and providing feedback on your book description, metadata, and author bios.

Here are some prompts to get you started with saving time on the title, bios, and description generation:

Prompt 1: I'm writing a book with a tentative title, "ChatGPT Millionaire: How to Automate & Generate 7 Streams of Passive Income". How could I make this title even more punchy and compelling? For audiences that are interested in passive income, what are some keywords I might want to consider including in my title?

Prompt 2: The following is my book description for an ebook I will publish called {Title} to help readers achieve {outcome}. Suggest three ways I can improve this description and better communicate the value my book will offer my readers.

Prompt 3: The following is my author bio for an ebook I will publish titled {Title} to help readers achieve {outcome}. Suggest three ways I can improve my author bio to communicate better how I am an experienced expert on the topic that can genuinely help my readers.

Conclusion

Last but certainly not least, self-publishing is a prime income stream to consider adding to your portfolio. Anyone can indeed get started. You don't have to be a writer. You don't have to have a degree. Exploring the infinite niches and creative angles you can take across different types of books, from low content to fantasy fiction, is enjoyable.

I love that self-publishing is a highly automatable business and that you can build it to generate truly passive income while also exploring your hobbies and interests and expressing your unique talents in the form of books that bring your readers joy, insight, and inspiration.

CONCLUSION

"It is good to have an end to journey toward; but it is the journey that matters, in the end." — *Ursula K. Le Guin*

What an incredible journey. From letting go of our limiting beliefs to embodying millionaire mindsets and diving right into ChatGPT and AI automation.

Identifying and letting go of our limiting beliefs is essential for our ongoing personal development on the journey to generating wealth for ourselves and our loved ones.

No matter how much we study the intricacies of finance, technology, and AI, if we have limiting beliefs, we will add massive friction to our wheels and blinders to our perspectives.

Cash flow equals energy flow, passive income vs active income, working on the business, not in the business. These are all millionaire mindsets to reconnect with and embody, shortcuts to the ultimate state of abundance we seek.

ChatGPT is an incredible technology we're only beginning to incorporate into our lives. Combining GPT with tools like Retool allows us to create complete end-to-end automations that can automate our businesses into genuinely passive income streams, allowing us to build and scale our income streams with ease.

As we explored different types of businesses to consider adding to our portfolio of passive income streams, we met many inspiring entrepreneurs along the way, from million-aire paranormal fiction self-published authors to bloggers exiting their businesses for $200 million. These entrepre-neurs show us that outstanding success is possible for anyone willing to put their minds to it and to put in the work.

I invite you to take the 7 Streams of Income Challenge to heart and see how you can generate and automate your seven income streams in 30 days. I am confident you can do it and create the financial freedom, abundance, and uncom-monly fine life you deserve.

> *"Our deepest fear is not that we are inadequate. Our deepest fear is that we are powerful beyond measure."* — *Marianne Williamson*

YOUR FREE GIFT

As a token of my gratitude for your recent purchase, I'm excited to offer you an exclusive copy of *108+ High Quality Passive Income Ideas* for free.

Get your free copy at bit.ly/108passiveincome.

Inside This Must-Read Guide, You'll Discover:

- **High Quality Passive Income Strategies:** An abundance of high-quality ideas to generate passive income.
- **Automatable Business Ideas:** Learn about various types of businesses that you can start and

automate for efficiency, ensuring a steady flow of income.

- **Smart Investment Ideas:** Explore a variety of investments you can make, as well as user-friendly investing platforms to grow your wealth.

Why You Shouldn't Miss This Opportunity:

- If you're aiming to diversify your income sources and build multiple passive income streams, this book is your key to unlocking those goals.
- Packed with real-world examples and success stories, it's more than just a book, this book suggests what may be uniquely possible for you.

Get Instant Access! Claim your free copy of **108+ High Quality Passive Income Ideas** *at bit.ly/108passiveincome.*

Thank you again for your purchase and I hope you enjoy the book!

BIBLIOGRAPHY

Alexander, J., & Pettingale, T. (2023). *Amazon.com: Self-Published Millionaire: The Step-by-Step Guide to Writing Publishing and Marketing Your First Book (How to Self Publish) eBook : Alexander, Joseph, Pettingale, Tim: Kindle Store.* Amazon.com. https://www.amazon.com/Self-Published-Millionaire-Step-Step-Publishing-ebook/dp/B07KB-SKS8B#:~:text=Joseph%20Alexander%20has%20set%20the,be-come%20a%20self%2Dpublished%20sensation.

Blakeley, K. (2011, July 15). Who Wants To Be A (Kindle) Millionaire? *Forbes.* https://www.forbes.com/sites/kiriblakeley/2011/03/06/who-wants-to-be-a-kindle-millionaire/?sh=338baabc1010

Burns, S. (2020, December 12). Why They Call This Entrepreneur The Millionaire Maker. *Forbes.* https://www.forbes.com/sites/stephanieburns/2020/12/04/why-they-call-this-entrepreneur-the-millionaire-maker/?sh=11dfa87728db

Consulting.com. (2023). *Consulting.com.* Consulting.com. https://www.consulting.com/

Corley, T. C. (2023). *Amazon.com: Rich Habits: The Daily Success Habits of Wealthy Individuals eBook : Corley, Thomas C. : Kindle Store.* Amazon.com. https://www.amazon.com/Rich-Habits-Success-Wealthy-Individuals-ebook/dp/B00IDJGVT4/ref=tmm_kin_swatch_0?_encod-ing=UTF8&qid=1698628800&sr=1-1

Dollwet, S. (2016). *About | Royaltyhero.* Royaltyhero. https://www.royalty-hero.com/about

Ermey, R. (2022, August 4). *30-year-old retiree earned $97,000 in passive income from Amazon last year: Here's how she got started.* CNBC; CNBC. https://www.cnbc.com/2022/08/04/this-millennial-earned-97000-last-year-from-two-self-published-books.html

Gerber, M. E. (2023). *Amazon.com: The E-Myth Revisited: Why Most Small Businesses Don't Work and What to Do About It (Audible Audio Edition): Michael E. Gerber, Michael E. Gerber, HarperAudio: Audible Books & Origi-nals.* Amazon.com. https://www.amazon.com/The-E-Myth-Revisited-audiobook/dp/B00094F0ES/ref=sr_1_1?crid=2YTW593I7016C&key-words=e-myth&qid=1698628788&sprefix=e-m%2Caps%2C158&sr=8-1

Heer, Dr. D., & Douglas, G. M. (2023). *Right Riches For You - Kindle edition by Douglas, Gary M. , Heer, Dr. Dain. Self-Help Kindle eBooks @ Amazon.com.*

Amazon.com. https://www.amazon.com/Right-Riches-You-Dain-Heer-ebook/dp/B00BA4JEDE/ref=sr_1_1?crid=3JTWOBUIECJOH&key-words=right+money+for+you+gary+douglas&qid=1698629169&s=digital-text&sprefix=right+money+for+you+gary+doug%2Cdigital-text%2C146&sr=1-1

Hunckler, M. (2017, April 14). How Brian Clark Built His Copyblogger Empire by Obsessing Over His Audience. *Forbes*. https://www.forbes.com/sites/matthunckler/2017/04/14/how-brian-clark-built-his-copyblogger-empire-by-obsessing-over-his-audience/?sh=31b3f87c702d

Kiyosaki, R. T. (2022, April 5). *Rich Dad Poor Dad: What the Rich Teach Their Kids About Money That the Poor and Middle Class Do Not!: Kiyosaki, Robert T.: 9781612681139: Amazon.com: Books*. Amazon.com. https://www.amazon.com/Rich-Dad-Poor-Teach-Middle/dp/1612681131/ref=sr_1_1?crid=14LVZPJCXRFM5&key-words=rich+dad+poor+dad&qid=1698628778&spre-fix=rich+dad+poor+d%2Caps%2C188&sr=8-1

Lardinois, F. (2023, September 7). *Low-code platform Retool makes it easier to bring AI smarts to business apps | TechCrunch*. TechCrunch. https://techcrunch.com/2023/09/07/low-code-platform-retool-makes-it-easier-to-bring-ai-smarts-to-business-apps/

Leslie, D. (2018). *Course From Scratch*. Coursefromscratch.com. https://join.coursefromscratch.com/

Leslie, D. (2020). *DANIELLE LESLIE (@danielleslie) • Instagram photos and videos*. Instagram.com. https://www.instagram.com/danielleslie/?hl=en

Lunden, I. (2022, July 28). *Retool raises $45M at a $3.2B valuation to make building custom software as easy as buying off the shelf | TechCrunch*. TechCrunch. https://techcrunch.com/2022/07/28/retool-raises-45m-at-a-3-2b-valuation-to-make-building-custom-software-as-easy-as-buying-off-the-shelf/

Malekos, N. (2023, May 10). *A.I. Course Creation: How to Use ChatGPT to Create eLearning Content*. LearnWorlds. https://www.learnworlds.com/chatgpt-create-online-courses/#brainstorm

Nerdynav. (2022, December 13). *107 Up-to-Date ChatGPT Statistics & User Numbers [Oct 2023]*. Nerdynav. https://nerdynav.com/chatgpt-statistics/

OpenAI. (2023). *GPT Best Practices*. Openai.com. https://platform.openai.com/docs/guides/gpt-best-practices

Retool. (2023a). *Retool apps | Retool Docs*. Retool.com. https://docs.retool.com/apps

Retool. (2023b). *Retool Workflows | Retool Docs*. Retool.com. https://docs.retool.com/workflows

Retool. (2023c). *Store documents and text in Retool Vectors | Retool Docs.* Retool.com. https://docs.retool.com/ai/guides/vectors/text

Robbins, T. (2021). *The ultimate guide to limiting beliefs from Tony Robbins.* Tonyrobbins.com. https://www.tonyrobbins.com/limiting-beliefs-guide/

Sabatier, G. (2018, March 13). *How To Make Money Blogging: Average Blogger Salary in 2023.* Millennial Money. https://millennialmoney.com/how-much-money-make-blogging/

Shubel, M. (2022, September). *How To Overcome Your Limiting Beliefs About Money.* Clever Girl Finance. https://www.clevergirlfinance.com/limiting-beliefs-about-money/

Siu, E. (2019, February 4). *GE 293: How Consulting.com Founder Sam Ovens' Course-Based Services Brought in $34 Million Last Year! (podcast).* Leveling Up. https://www.levelingup.com/growth-everywhere-interview/sam-ovens-consulting-dot-com/

Todorov, G. (2021, July 15). *How Much do Bloggers Make in 2023? [Real and Amazing Stats].* Learn Digital Marketing. https://thrivemyway.com/how-much-bloggers-make/

van Tongeren, R. (2018, June 27). *This Is How 10 Bloggers in Different Niches Make $1 Million+ per Year • Smart Blogger.* Smart Blogger. https://smart-blogger.com/million-dollar-bloggers/

Made in United States
North Haven, CT
11 February 2024

48595575R00085